11/05/84

Dear Ellie...

You're the cheese in my omelet

Happy cooking and regards

Howard

The
40-SECOND OMELET
Guaranteed

The Gourmet Way to Breakfast,

Brunch, Lunch, Dinner

and Dessert

by HOWARD HELMER
with Joan O'Sullivan

The
40-SECOND OMELET
Guaranteed

ATHENEUM   NEW YORK   1982

ILLUSTRATED BY ALISON POTTER

Library of Congress Cataloging in Publication Data

Helmer, Howard.
The 40-second omelet guaranteed

Includes index.
　　1. Cookery (Eggs)　I. O'Sullivan, Joan.　II. Title.
III. Title: Forty-second omelet guaranteed
TX745.H44　　641.6′75　　81-70072
ISBN 0-689-11288-2　　　AACR2

Copyright © 1982 by Howard Helmer and Joan O'Sullivan
Illustrations copyright © 1982 by Atheneum Publishers, Inc.
All rights reserved
Published simultaneously in Canada by McClelland and
　　Stewart Ltd.
Composed by American–Stratford Graphic Services, Inc.,
　　Brattleboro, Vermont
Manufactured by Fairfield Graphics, Fairfield, Pennsylvania
Designed by Mary Cregan
First Edition

With love and appreciation to my wife, Sonni,
and my sons Michael and Gordon
who helped hatch my career and,
in the process, have racked up
their own records for omelet eating.

Contents

Acknowledgments

Special thanks to Arlene Wanderman for her untiring
help with recipes and creative food ideas. Thanks
also to Maryann White and Jim Reiter whose overtime efforts kept this book organized and accurate.
And to the American Egg Board who not only taught
me everything I know about P/R but opened their
recipe files to me in assembling material for this book.

The
40-SECOND OMELET
Guaranteed

1.

How and Why I Became the World's Fastest Omelet-Maker

From the dawn of culinary history, the world's most successful chefs have been men blessed with superb digital dexterity and superhuman hand-eye coordination. I am the exception. I'm a klutz in the kitchen. I always have been. I always will be.

Most of my friends aren't aware of this grave shortcoming. That's because I've developed a specialty: I make fabulous omelets. It camouflages my native ineptitude, and it has given me a reputation as a great cook. If my friends ever thought about it, they'd realize that whatever the occasion when I invite them over—breakfast, brunch, lunch, dinner, or dessert—my menu does not change. It's omelets each and every time.

I don't know how to cook anything else.

I have an omelet fixation. You would, too, if, like me, you had been led to pop fame, a certain amount of fortune, and immortality—a listing in *The Guinness Book of World Records*—by the omelet.

I guess from the beginning, ham (that's me) and eggs were meant for each other. I must have had a hankering for show biz because when I met Rudy Stanish in 1972 I was dazzled.

Rudy was a New York celebrity. No posh party was complete unless Rudy catered, doing his omelet-making act before black-tie audiences whose faces were as familiar as their names. If you saw the Broadway show *Applause*, you'll remember that Rudy was mentioned in the script. Like James Beard, Jacques Pepin, and Julia Child, he, too, cooked for an audience . . . and the audience paid through the nose for the privilege.

Rudy's expertise lay not only in his ability to make superb omelets but in his technique: He made it look as easy as putting together an atom bomb. Like Fred Astaire performing a dance number, Rudy had mystique when it came to whipping up an omelet. He boogied in front of his fire, shaking his special omelet pan with one hand, twirling his special omelet fork with the other, rolling the omelet in a special manner that cried out for great fanfare.

Were you the seventh son of the seventh son of the world's greatest juggler, you had the feeling you couldn't hope to duplicate the Rudy Stanish omelet-making technique.

So imagine my surprise when Rudy took me as a student. He promised to teach me all his tricks, so that I, too, could become a celebrated cook working audiences culled straight from the Celebrity Register.

This is my big chance, I thought, and agreed to put on an apron and submit to omelet-making lessons, two in all. In neither did I get my left hand and right hand in sync.

"There's nothing to it," Rudy assured me. "Watch me in action."

He had me help out at a black-tie party in the duplex apartment of H. Drew Heinz (of the Heinz 57 Varieties clan) at River House, one of Manhattan's poshest addresses. The party followed the opening of the Broadway show, *Joe Egg*. Mrs. Heinz had decided there was no better menu for her first-nighter guests at *Joe Egg* than eggs—in Rudy Stanish omelets.

I rented a tux and polished my only pair of shoes. They were brown.

My first setback: I was led to the kitchen where I was asked to shed my tux jacket. I put on an apron and broke eggs by the dozens.

There was no glamour in this, so I really got cracking and did the job at jet speed so I could re-don my tux, mix, mingle, and meet.

For a naive, brown-shoed Chicago boy like myself who'd been in New York less than a year, the guest list was nothing less than overwhelming. I hobnobbed with Albert Finney, star of *Joe Egg*. I exchanged small talk with Doug Fairbanks, Greta Garbo, Mary Martin, and Josh Logan. Before long I was convinced I was on

5

a stage set. The living room was two stories high. It had floor-to-ceiling windows, lush draperies, and an elegant stairway leading to a balcony. I decided I was probably in the lobby of the Plaza Hotel, entertaining Scott and Zelda. There was an East River view that looked like an Andy Warhol painting capturing, as it did, a giant red neon sign advertising Pepsi Cola.

Clearly I had arrived. Then I was summoned back to the kitchen.

The house lights went down, the audience gathered, and Rudy Stanish began his omelet-making act, a star with a supporting cast of one—me. A conscientious observer.

I stood behind a long table, in the shadows, serving omelets as fast as Rudy made them. In no time at all, my newfound friends were handing me their dirty dishes. I guess I cracked when a celebrated society matron whose name was synonymous with big bucks approached. Only 30 minutes before, she'd been "deee-lighted" to meet me. Now she handed me her cigarette butt to snuff out.

I piled up the dirty dishes behind the two-story-high draperies, put on my tux jacket, and left. Catering wasn't for me.

But I had learned something: How to make an omelet the hard way—with French pizzazz.

Little did I think then that this bit of knowledge would make a profound change in my life. For soon I became a publicist, my employer the American Egg Board.

One day egg producers and their wives were having a big bash at the Concord Hotel in the Catskills. My assignment: Keep the wives entertained while their husbands conferred. The original plan had been for me to show the ladies a film, *Small Wonder,* wherein a character called "Super Egg" (no relation to "Joe Egg") tells his story. But it was a film made for schoolchildren. I thought a group of smart chicks would be bored by it and decided to do my Rudy Stanish impression. I'd make omelets and show them how to do it.

It wasn't easy—all the twirling, rolling, and coordinating. The women found it entertaining. Personally, I loved being in the spotlight.

The session worked out so successfully that I took my show on the road as a promotion for the Egg Board. I played women's clubs, B'nai B'rith, Rosary Societies, the DAR—you name it.

What an ego egg trip! Then one day I realized something was missing. Mine was a great act to watch—but most of the women in my audiences were intimidated by my performance. I made making omelets look too hard. In truth, the way I made omelets then, it wasn't easy. Whenever I invited volunteers from the audience to come up and try, they failed. They couldn't get the shake, rattle, and roll of it all.

In the meantime, I had become slightly sick of fine-chopping cheese, bacon, and chives. When you "roll" an omelet, the filling ingredients used have to be itsy-bitsy. Actually, it was more a knick-knack situation—my fingers were knicked because I lacked the knack of chopping. My chest wasn't broad enough for all the purple hearts I earned in those days.

That's when I remembered the times I used to watch my grandmother making blintzes. The same technique would work for omelets, I thought. And the 40-second, no-nonsense, no-frill omelet was on the verge of discovery.

Just one thing stood in my way: the shaking. Of course you had to shake an omelet, otherwise it would stick to the pan like Miss Melanie clinging to Ashley Wilkes. Modern technology saved my day: sticking was eliminated by no-stick pan coating. Had I only been in a bathtub, I would have shouted, "Eureka!" Like Archimedes, I, too, had discovered a principle! Even more important, I had found an easy way to enjoy my favorite combination: eggs, French fries, and American cheese—not gourmet but good. I'd place the ingredients atop the omelet and *fold* the omelet instead of rolling it—no fine chopping needed.

A star was born—ME!

I wouldn't just demonstrate, I'd let selected members of the audience come up and make 40-second omelets, proving how easy it was. I'd bring my message to the cooks of America, and teach everyone the easy art of omelet-making.

Anne Spaeth, then manager of the Congressional Club in Washington, D.C., whose membership includes wives of senators, congressmen, and cabinet members, took my idea a step further. She just wasn't impressed by the program.

"Why only one or two from the audience?" she asked. "Why not let everyone make an omelet?"

"Because if we use hot plates, we'll blow every fuse in the Capitol," I said, "and the FBI will think I'm subversive."

Still, the idea of an omelet-making spectacular had appeal. How could I swing it? There must be a way.

I did some research and discovered table burners that operated on butane gas instead of electricity.

Anne and I worked out the logistics. For every ten people, we needed one burner, one bucket of 20 eggs mixed with water, bowls of ham, cheese, and mushrooms for filling, one ladle, one spatula, and a stack of warm plates. I estimated that since an omelet cooks in 40 seconds, even allowing a full minute per person, 100 people using 10 burners could each cook an omelet within a total time of 10 minutes.

With Anne's help, my omelet-making show was ready to hit the road. All I needed to do was polish up my act. Even Milton Berle couldn't dazzle them in 40 seconds. I couldn't do songs but I could do patter.

I worked up an amusing history of the egg and practiced a show-stopper, making a flaming omelet because everyone likes a good fire at the dinner table. I'd get some help from the audience by asking, "Anyone here who burns salad?" And I'd recruit a straight man.

At long last, I was where I belonged—in show biz—and my employer, the American Egg Board, couldn't have been happier. I was in demand. People actually wanted to book my act.

Thousands of omelets later, I found myself playing the Pennsylvania Farm Show in Harrisburg to an SRO audience. Actually, they didn't care about omelet-making. They wanted to eat the omelets and, Lord knows, there were lots of them. As a publicity gimmick, I'd decided to break the *Guinness Book* record for omelet-making. To lend credibility, extension specialists armed with official stopwatches and with degrees in animal husbandry were in attendance to swear to my achievement. We were following the *Guinness Book* requirements to the letter—or so I thought.

There was lots of hoopla and lots of press coverage as I broke the world record, making more than 184 omelets in the specified 30 minutes, more than the *Guinness* record holder had.

BUT—he had made plain omelets! I'd made cheese-filled ones, which definitely was harder. But *Guinness* decreed that I hadn't broken his record.

I got temperamental and vowed never to try again. If the *Guinness* people didn't know a star when they saw one—tough.

Meanwhile, back to all the omelets I'd cooked. A crowd was clamoring for them, as they stretched as far as the eye could see on a table that seemed to stretch forever. It was free-lunch time. But the flies that had followed the livestock to the farm-show building where I'd done my *eggstravaganza* had beaten the crowd to them. The omelets looked like black dotted Swiss. Lest we start some sort of epidemic, the local Board of Health gathered up the omelets and recycled them as feed for the chickens, who'd lay more eggs that would become more omelets. I began to feel part of Nature's grand scheme. The egg and I were symbiotic.

Still, I sulked. I'd given my all—cooked more than 184 filled omelets on 6 burners in 30 minutes—only to be snubbed. I would never, ever go through such torture again.

I did in 1978, for a very good reason. The American Egg Board was opening the American Egg House restaurant in Disneyland, in Anaheim, California. They wanted to turn it into a happening. They wanted headlines!

But I was by then not only fast with a skillet, I was now the head of my own public relations agency, Food Communications, Inc., and I knew what I had to do: Cook on all burners and break *The Guinness Book of World Records* record, this time officially. It was do or die. I knew I could do.

I probably broke another world record, too. Never, ever has anyone, anywhere cracked as many eggs as I did while I trained for the main event. I cracked and cooked for four hours a week for four weeks. In fighting trim, I flew to American Egg Board headquarters in Chicago for a dress rehearsal. They didn't want egg on their faces if I failed. I didn't. It was all systems go!

On July 14, 1978, while an unsuspecting world waited, I revved up for record-breaking. It began with a parade down Disneyland's main drag—Mickey Mouse and me, Goofy, Dumbo, and some of the seven

dwarfs. There was the Disneyland Band playing the "Incredible, Edible Egg" of TV and radio commercial fame, and there was me, raring to go.

As thousands cheered, I whipped up 217 plain omelets in 30 minutes. Mickey Mouse crowned me with a chef's toque emblazoned with the message: "World's Champion Omelet Maker." Someone stuck a sign in the 184th world record-breaking omelet. But, alas, no one saved and bronzed that omelet for me. I'd planned to use it for an ash tray.

Immortality was mine—there I was enshrined for posterity, an entry in the *Guinness Book,* forever sandwiched between Noodle Twisting and Flapjack Flipping. At last I had made my mother proud.

Actually, I could have cooked more omelets but once I broke the record with my 184th, I held back. Like every title holder, I've got reserves so I can best any challengers. No one has yet come forth. I can't imagine why.

Maybe it's not the Nobel Prize, but who cares. I like autographing the *Guinness Book.* "You're the cheese in my omelet," I'll write. Or "I hope all of your dreams—and omelets—pan out."

Winning that record gave me cachet. I've cooked my way around the U.S., demonstrating omelet-making for the nation's VIP's. They're all astonished. I've taught the greatest—more politicians, more secretaries of agriculture, more senators and congressmen than you could shake an omelet pan at—*if* you cooked omelets the difficult French way and not the easy Howard Helmer way. Not to mention the celebrities—Rock Hudson, Dinah Shore, Angie Dickinson, Steve Lawrence, Eydie Gorme, Lucille Ball, Dave de Busschere, and Jimmy Stewart included. Jimmy just said, "Aw shucks." He was my only failure. But while Jimmy was "Aw shucksing" I was making another omelet. It's that quick and that easy—as you'll discover in the chapters that follow.

2.

In Case You Wondered Which Came First . . .

Philosophers have always asked profound questions:

> "Is the world round?"
> "Did the universe begin with a bang or a whimper?"
> "Which came first, the chicken or the egg?"

I'm no Einstein, yet I sometimes wonder why so many people have wasted so much time puzzling about the last one. That the question was raised at all indicates something: The chicken and the egg rate high in the eternal pecking order. After all, the fateful question might have been: "What came first, the cow or the

calf, the frog or the tad, the silkworm or the butterfly?"

But it's the chicken and the egg that have caused whiz kids down through the ages to scratch their heads, stroke their beards, wear solemn expressions, and ponder.

Didn't any of them ever read their Bible? The answer is right there in Genesis 1:20 for all to see: "And God said, Let the waters bring forth abundantly the moving creatures that hath life, and fowl that may fly above the earth in the open firmament of Heaven."

So the chicken came first, fast followed by the egg, which led to more chickens and more eggs and eventually to my doing what I had to do to rate a mention in *The Guinness Book of World Records.*

Down through history, the egg has gotten better billing than the chicken that laid it. There it was, gift wrapped by Mother Nature in a perfect package, the original sex symbol. When the ancients thought about eggs, they were thinking about reproduction. Its shell was symbolic of life, its white of water, its yolk of fire, and the area under its shell of air. The egg to them meant life—and what's life without sex?

By the time the Druids dipped into eggs, they weren't dealing with hens but with serpents, which they considered symbolic of power and success. Serpents' eggs could be powerful but I doubt their success in my omelet pan.

Painted eggs, the kind the Easter Bunny brings, began not as a symbol of the Resurrection but as a Chinese custom in 722 BC, when it was decreed that in honor of the Spring Festival all fires in the province of Kingts-oo were to be put out and remain out for three days. One provident chieftain, probably a member of the local Tammany Hall, came up with a way to make friends and influence people. He amassed a great store of painted eggs, dispensing them to his constituency for the duration. History doesn't record whether they were hard boiled or not but anyone as savvy as that Chinese pol must have figured out that hard boiled keep and travel better. And if you're going to the trouble of painting them, you don't want your eggs cracking up.

The Persians had a similar custom. Jemsheed, the mystical monarch, sixth in descent from Moses, gave travelers dyed eggs each spring during a feast marking the beginning of the religious year.

In the twelfth century the French had a tradition calling for the bride to step on an egg as she crossed the threshold of her new home. This assured good luck and also introduced her to the idea of spending time on her hands and knees.

Given an egg or two, I can predict I'm going to make breakfast, brunch, lunch, dinner, or dessert. In Roman times, they thought an egg could predict a great deal more. For example, an oracle told Livia, the future wife of Roman Emperor Augustus, that if she'd carry an egg in the warmth between her breasts, the sex of her unborn child would be indicated by whether a male or female chick was hatched. Thanks to this advice, Tiberius was born and the recent television success of "I, Claudius" guaranteed.

Tiberius didn't have too much to crow about since his rule led to the moral deterioration of the empire.

But he is credited with making the first omelet. (The Chinese, though, were said to be making a sort of Egg Foo Yung—an oriental Denver or Western omelet—centuries before.) Nobody knows for sure what his recipe was, but Tiberius' omelet was filled with honey.

It took centuries for the French to take hold of the idea, develop it, refine it, and give it some flair. It is thought that the omelet moved to France with one of the many Italian chefs who migrated to France in the fifteenth century when the age of haute cuisine was born.

The thrifty French saw in the *omelette* a great vehicle for leftovers that couldn't be held in those pre-refrigeration days. Eggs wrapped themselves neatly around any other food and completely changed the complexion of what was inside. Yesterday's supper could take on new color, shape, and form. It was even hidden from view so it wouldn't be recognizable.

Some other classic French egg dishes probably were created for the same practical purpose—to camouflage leftovers. For example, the soufflé is a béchamel into which leftovers may be mixed. It's then baked into what we now consider a crowning culinary achievement when all it really is a Puff of Leftovers.

The quiche is nothing more than a custard pie into which almost any other food may be mixed. Americans who couldn't spell "quiche" figured they couldn't make one. Had it been called Odds-and-Ends Pie, they'd have tried it pronto and discovered it's a cinch to bring off.

Ditto for the crêpe, a smaller, thinner omeletlike

pancake that can be rolled around almost any kind of food. Few Americans made crêpes while they were pronounced the French way to rhyme with "preps." It wasn't until someone starting calling them "kraypes" that they caught on and a full-fledged fad for Left-overs-in-a-Blanket swept the U.S.

Lots of superstitions surround the egg and if you're superstitious, it's okay by me. Personally—knock on wood—I don't believe you can break a spell by passing an egg back and forth before the face of the bewitched, breaking the egg, checking out its yolk (who knows for what), then burying it in a secret place. It seems like a lot of trouble and a great waste of good egg.

I do believe in one piece of good luck—getting an egg with two yolks. How could that be anything but lucky when eggs taste so good!

The Scottish used eggs for fortune-telling, which is a messier mystical technique than reading tea leaves, but to each his own. They broke the first egg laid by a pullet into a glass of water, then looked for clues about what was to come in the formation of the egg white.

My favorite portion of egg lore is the French belief that the 100 pleats on a chef's toque represent 100 ways to prepare eggs. But 100 is a modest figure when it comes to variations on the omelet, as we shall see.

3.

Everything You Thought You Needed to Know About Omelet-Making, but Don't

I call it cooking. Food snobs call it cuisine. And therein lies the difference. They spell their dishes in French to one-up their friends even before they turn on the stove.

Take a dish like the omelet. By spelling it "omelette," the food snobs create sophistication and complexity. I spell omelets the way I make them—simple.

"Approach omelette-making with confidence," suggests a French cookbook author, the implication being that unknown perils lie ahead.

But omelet-making doesn't require any more confidence than boiling water.

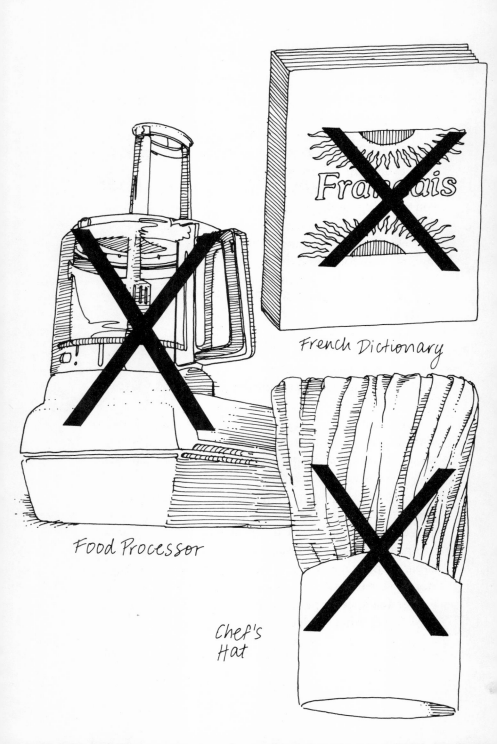

French Dictionary

Food Processor

Chef's
Hat

It is not difficult, involved, complicated, doomed to failure or dependent on mystic rites. It really is as simple as boiling, scrambling, frying, or poaching eggs. You'd never guess this from reading a French cookbook or talking to a French gourmet or chef. All imply that, even with a Cordon Bleu diploma in hand, your chances for a successful outcome would be better were you paddling up the Zambezi followed by a canoe load of angry natives.

Well, forget everything you've heard about omelet-making from food snobs.

For starters, let's consider what's *not* needed in the way of special equipment. Remember, we're getting ready to cook a couple of eggs, not assembling a Swiss watch.

You do *not* need a special, reserved-for-omelets-only pan that has been seasoned for months. That's the kind of propaganda that contributes to omelet-making jitters.

All you need is a regular 8- or 10-inch frying pan with sloping sides and a nonstick coating called Silverstone. Silverstone keeps the eggs from sticking and leaves you free to concentrate on just one thing: how your omelet is coming along. The fact that you fried potatoes in the pan for breakfast or used it to cook a burger for lunch doesn't mean a thing. Such a pan is inexpensive and universally available in housewares departments, hardware stores, supermarkets, drugstores, department stores, and discount stores. So: Forget the special pan. Forget the special seasoning. And forget what you've heard about shaking the pan and doing a spectacular number "rolling" the omelet. You're going to "fold" the omelet instead, and that technique's a snap.

Originally, a certain amount of razzle-dazzle was practical. Chefs had to do a boogie and shake the pan because it didn't have a nonstick coating. If they stopped shaking, the egg would stick to the bottom.

In addition to being much simpler to do, folding the omelet has two distinct advantages over rolling. First, if you damage the four-star appearance of your omelet, say by tearing it with your spatula, it doesn't matter because in the folding method the omelet winds up face down on the plate—the torn top side out of view.

Secondly, when you roll an omelet, the filling you use has to be finely chopped or diced—too much work. Since a folded omelet accepts bulk, you can use whole asparagus spears, potato slices, broccoli rosettes, or other such fillings. The folded omelet full of things looks better and is more nourishing.

Forget "omelette" mystique. Think of what the omelet really is: a pocket waiting to be filled, a sandwich waiting to be spread, an almost instant and exceedingly easy meal. I guarantee it.

4.

The 40-Second Secret

There are some things even your best friend won't tell you—like the special super spice she puts in herb bread. And, for awhile, that's probably how you'll feel about the 40-second omelet-making secret I'm about to divulge.

It's so easy, it's almost embarrassing to reveal it. Enjoy it as a secret for awhile, then share the good news . . . and make a friend forever.

You don't even need a pencil to jot down the magic formula. It's as easy to recall as your phone number. In fact, it's easier. So here goes for the recipe:

40-SECOND OMELET

> *2 eggs*
> *2 tablespoons of water*

Got that? Good! Beat it briefly with a fork.

Remember: 2 eggs and 2 tablespoons of water make 1 fluffy, fabulous omelet. That's all there basically is to it except for the filling. Plenty of suggestions for fillings that will turn 2 eggs and 2 tablespoons of water into breakfast, brunch, lunch, dinner or dessert follow.

Don't take liberties with the basic formula and assume that if 2 eggs and 2 tablespoons of water make 1 omelet you can mix 10 eggs and 10 tablespoons of water and come up with a giant omelet that'll serve 5. It doesn't work that way. If you want to serve 5, make 5 individual omelets, each containing (repeat after me) 2 eggs and 2 tablespoons of water.

If that sounds difficult—making 5 small omelets instead of 1 king size—look at it this way: It'll take you slightly more than 3 minutes to make 5 (40-second) omelets. In fact, you can have 'em done while you're reading this. There is a little method to this omelet madness—but not much.

To make 5 omelets, what you do is mix those 10 eggs and 10 tablespoons of water in a big bowl. But how will you know how much is 2 eggs and 2 tablespoons of water to make each of 5 omelets?

I thought you'd never ask!

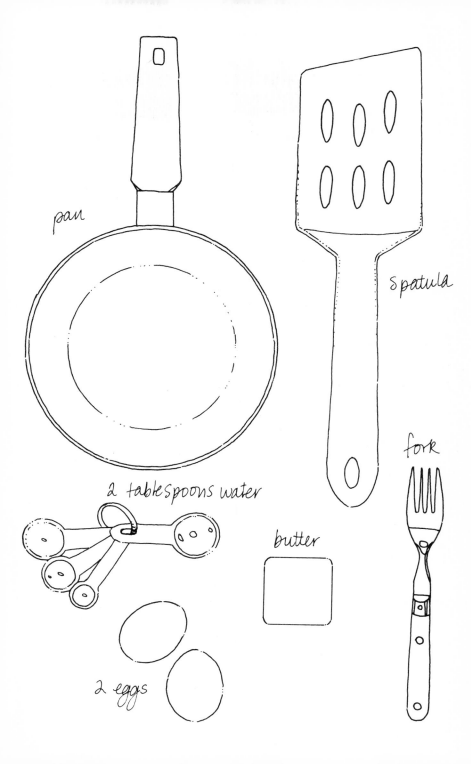

pan

spatula

fork

2 tablespoons water

butter

2 eggs

You'll know because a standard kitchen soup ladle (½ cup measure) holds exactly 2 eggs and 2 table-spoons of water. I sometimes marvel at the wonder of this. Maybe when the first ladle was being designed and was sitting on a kitcheneer's drawing board as he pondered the big question, "How much should I make this ladle hold?" it was like God said, "Make the ladle hold 2 eggs and 2 tablespoons of water," because that's how the ladle turned out. And thank God for that.

THE 40-SECOND TECHNIQUE

Whether you're making 1 omelet or 5, the technique's the same. Here's what you do for each one:

Get your pan hot. Just on the brink of smoking.

Now I know some of you readers have had Home Economics 101, and in Home Ec 101 you learned never to expose eggs to high heat because it toughens them up. Like all rules, this one has an exception. The 40-second omelet is it. Those eggs are in and out of that hot pan so quick they never know what hit them. The eggs' protein fibers don't get a chance to toughen because the egg is constantly in motion for those 40 fast seconds.

A hot pan is best, but if the idea makes you nervous, switch down to moderate heat. If high is a 10 on your stove, cook your omelet at 8. It will just take a second or two longer to cook, that's all.

So start with a hot or medium-hot pan, then take a pat (about a tablespoon) of butter and put it in the pan. You don't need the butter to keep the egg from sticking in a Silverstone-coated pan. You use the butter for just one reason: to flavor the eggs.

Put the butter in the pan and, quick before it burns, add a ladle full of egg mix and look what happens: The whole thing bursts into bubbles. You know what the bubbles are? Those bubbles are the water in the egg mix turning to steam and evaporating, leaving big air pockets in the egg. Those air pockets are what makes the omelet light and puffy.

That's why you've got to use water in an omelet—not milk. Yes, you can use milk, cream, even cream cheese or mayonnaise in scrambled eggs which call for a thick, rich mixture, where the egg is conspicuous and not as inconspicuous as it is in an omelet. But you can't use them in an omelet, no sirree.

WHY MILK IS A NO-NO

If you use milk in an omelet, the milk will curdle the second it hits that hot pan and the eggs are going to lie there, heavy as an elephant's foot. And you're going to have an omelet that just doesn't rise to the occasion and is going to taste tough.

So you've got to use water because water is what turns to steam, evaporates, makes air pockets and results in a puffy end product on your plate.

COOKING YOUR OMELET

There's a simple reason why an omelet takes 40 seconds to cook: All of the egg that hits the surface of the pan is instantly cooked. That's because the pan's surface is hot. But not all of the egg is on the pan's surface. Some is sitting on top, saying "Cook me, cook me." So take a spatula or pancake turner, invert it, and, working in from the perimeter of the pan where the egg is set, simply move the cooked egg aside, pulling it toward the center of the pan. Then tilt the pan a little —no need to shake, rattle, or roll it—and the uncooked egg will pour into place, hitting the bare surface of the pan, and it will start cooking instantly. You just keep doing this, moving the cooked egg to the center, revealing a naked pan surface, then tilting so the uncooked egg pours onto the exposed pan until your entire omelet is cooked. Do big swooping sweeps with the spatula. The more pan surface you expose with each swoosh, the more egg you cook, and the quicker your omelet will be done. Remember, you're clocking it for 40 seconds flat.

For example, look down on the round pan as if it were a clock. I always start at the 12 o'clock position. I pull the egg toward the center of the pan—quickly, with one swoop—while simultaneously tilting the pan handle upward so the uncooked egg flows onto the bared pan surface even as I move the cooked egg aside. Then I quickly move to the 3 o'clock position, dragging the cooked egg toward the pan center while tilting the pan upward toward my right to allow more uncooked egg onto that bared pan surface. Then 6 o'clock. Then 9 o'clock.

There is a similar technique which I have found to work equally well. Rather than swooping the egg toward the center and tilting the pan, you may try lifting the cooked egg with a spatula around the perimeter of the pan, allowing the raw egg to flow underneath. This will take you a few seconds longer.

Word of Warning: Keep an eye on that omelet. Don't overcook it. Stop swooshing around with the spatula when it's light, fluffy, and no longer very runny. It should be moist on top, though, because it's going to go right on cooking when you get it out of the pan —that's why you should serve it on a warm but not hot plate.

I like my omelets very moist, so I stop swooshing the spatula around when there's still plenty of uncooked egg on top. It'll cook and set a lot more by the time I'm done filling and folding the omelet, taking it out of the pan and putting it on the plate.

FILLING, FOLDING, AND FLIPPING THE OMELET

So your omelet looks about ready and now it's time to do a very important thing: Turn the handle of the

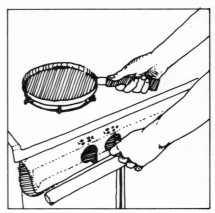
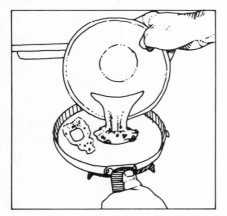

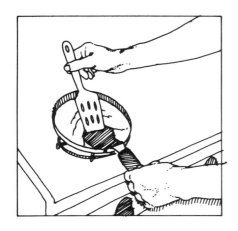
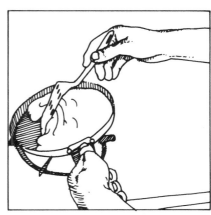
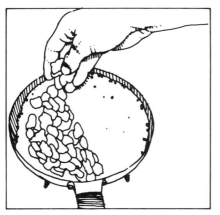
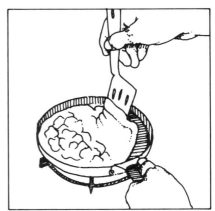

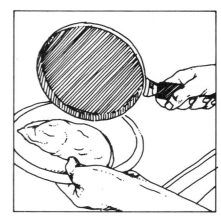

pan so it is pointed directly at your navel. The reason this is important is that you're going to fill the omelet on one side, fold the other side over the filling, and turn the whole thing upside down onto a plate. If the handle of the pan is pointed at 3 or 4 o'clock and you fill and fold the omelet, you'll have a helluva time turning the pan to flip the omelet upside down onto the plate because the omelet will fall out on your hand or the handle.

So make sure the handle of the pan is pointed right at your navel.

Now it's time to fill the omelet. You've got the filling chopped, sliced, whatever, and ready to spoon or fork onto the omelet. The instructions from here on in are for the righthanded, so, if you're a lefty, just reverse the directions which follow.

All of the filling, no matter how fine-chopped or bulky it is, goes on the lefthand side of the omelet. As you face the pan and the omelet, draw an imaginary line down the pan from 12 o'clock to 6 o'clock, and fill only to the left of that line. If you're using cheese, the cheese should be put in first, right against the hot surface of the omelet, because you want it to melt. Then top it with whatever else is in your super-filling combo. While both the top and bottom of the omelet will generate a lot of heat when the omelet is folded, they won't generate enough heat to cook foods. So all omelet fillings should be precooked and at room temperature or warmer.

Now you're ready to fold the omelet. Pick up your spatula, holding it as you would if sipping soup at the

Four Seasons restaurant. In other words, don't clasp the handle with a fist, then dig into the omelet. Hold it gingerly so it rests on your third finger and is supported by your thumb, then slide it all the way under the unfilled side of the omelet. Don't be timid. Don't even be afraid of tearing the omelet. It doesn't matter if you do —I'll explain why in a second. Get the spatula all the way under the omelet and fold, don't flip it. Lift the unfilled side over the filled side, right on top of the filling. (Remember, lefties, to reverse the directions and fill the right side of the omelet, folding the left side over the filling.) Use elbow action, not wrist action. Stick your elbow up in the air. The omelet always folds, except when it doesn't. When it doesn't, it tears. It's very difficult for a beginner to fold an omelet in one piece.

If you tear the omelet as you fold, don't worry. What's so great about an omelet is, no matter how you mess it up in the folding, it lands upside down on the plate so your mistake doesn't show.

Now you're ready to help that omelet out of the pan. Put down your spatula. You'll have no further use for it.

At this point, the handle of the pan should be pointed at your right hand and you should have a ready and waiting plate to the left of the pan.

Hold the plate in your left hand, and take the handle of the pan in your right hand and simply invert the pan so the omelet flips down on the plate, upside down.

Voila! as they say at the Cordon Bleu, a perfect omelet. And you did it in 40 seconds. Topside, it will look like a *Ladies' Home Journal* centerfold. And who cares about bottomside. Nobody ever sees it.

Traditionally, an omelet should look soft and creamy yellow when it lands on the plate. Alas, many people flinch at the thought of runny eggs and would prefer their omelets very well done. Even dry. For those people, I recommend that the butter be browned in the pan before the egg is added. The egg will brown from the butter rather than turning to the consistency of rubber, which is what happens to eggs when exposed to too much heat for too long a time.

You can go on and on and on, making one omelet after another—your second, third, fourth, fifth, all so picture perfect you'll wish you'd invited more guests, because if there's one thing a star like you needs, it's an audience.

5.

Omelets for Breakfast and Brunch

When it comes to omelets, don't put all your eggs in one basket. Diversify. Breakfast is a good place to begin because the egg is a traditional start-the-day food. Eggs are forever linked to breakfast because day begins at cock's crow—and eggs give a rooster something to crow about.

Whatever the reason, the season, or the number you're serving, an omelet's a cinch to whip up with your eyes shut—as mine often are until my third cup of coffee.

So let me egg you on. For a quick and easy breakfast or brunch, whip up a 40-second omelet with a spe-

cial filling. My favorites for breakfast and brunch follow.

Important: Remember that ½ to ⅓ cup of filling is sufficient for 1 omelet, although some people, including me, think more is better! Filling should be hot or, at the minimum, room temperature, so warm up ingredients you've just removed from the fridge. The heat of the omelet will do the rest.

THE BREAKFAST AND BRUNCH OMELET

How do you tell what meal to serve which omelet at? It's not a high-level decision because I'll let you in on a secret: Breakfast, brunch, lunch, and dinner omelets are virtually interchangeable. It's what you serve with them that makes the difference: toast or English muffins for breakfast; a salad and rolls for lunch; a vegetable, salad, and hot French bread for dinner.

Still, some fillings seem more breakfast-y than others. Among them:

Bacon

Bacon and eggs go together like Antony and Cleopatra. But why stop there? Crumble 2 slices of cooked bacon over half the omelet, then add a handful of shredded Cheddar, Switzerland Swiss, or Gruyère.

Another great combo: bacon and diced tomatoes with a dollop of sour cream.

Bickford's restaurant chain, popular with New York's stay-up-all-night crowd during the forties and fifties, used to offer a breakfast special: one fried egg with pan-fried potatoes, applesauce, an English muffin, and two strips of bacon for under $1. The menu egged me on to new heights in omelet-making. I slice the potatoes chip-thin, fry them briefly, then use with crumbled bacon as omelet filling. The applesauce and English muffins are great go-withs.

Cheese

Any kind of cheese or any combination of cheeses is great in an omelet. I've used them all—Muenster, Swiss, mozzarella, provolone, Armenian string cheese, Gouda—grated, diced, shredded, in wafer-thin slices, solo or combined with bacon, ham, sausage.

Cream cheese has possibilities, too. Pimiento-stuffed olives and cream cheese, my favorite sandwich filling, make a great filling. Fine-chop the olives, then mix into soft cream cheese.

(*see Olives, page 55*)

Creamy cottage cheese (about ½ cup) is excellent in omelets. Try mixing it with a little well-drained cooked spinach and a pinch of nutmeg or dill.

Another trick: Try adding ⅛ teaspoon of crushed basil to the egg mix before cooking. Fill the omelet with a mixture of chopped chives or parsley and cottage cheese.

Fruit

Apples, peaches, pears, bananas, strawberries, and blueberries are super omelet fillers. Thin-slice or purée 'em. Another trick: Heat in the smallest amount of water (just enough to keep from burning), then spoon on the omelet piping hot, sugaring or not as you prefer.

(*see individual fruit listings in Chapter 8*)

Ham

Ham is heavenly. Serve as is or spread with horse-radish or seasoned mustard.

Jam

Something sweet often hits the spot for breakfast. If there's no Danish around to dunk in your coffee mug, try a jammed-up omelet, spreading 2 to 3 tablespoons of your favorite preserve over half the omelet. Fold, then sprinkle with a dusting of confectioners sugar.

(*see Peanut Butter, page 43*)

Onions

Fried onions can solo in an omelet or can combine with melted Casere, a Greek cheese that's heavenly when heated briefly until melted in a frying pan. Or try

onions with cheese and potatoes. I prefer onions in thick rings rather than diced for omelets.

(*also see Vegetables, page 44*)

Peanut Butter

If you're the kind of mother who says "Eat already" to a resistant kid morning, noon, and night, relax. Do I have a surefire formula for you. Instead of peanut butter and jelly sandwiches, serve PB & J as omelet filling. Wow! It's breakfast, brunch, lunch, dinner, or a super snack. It's a way out of cooking for you because even a kid can make an omelet. Use about 2 tablespoons peanut butter mixed with 1 to 2 tablespoons of jam or jelly. Guaranteed: The omelet won't stick to the roof of his mouth!

(*see Jam, page 41*)

Sausage

Some like it hot, some like it sweet, some like the brown-and-serve variety. I like omelets filled with sausage and:

- Piping hot kidney beans
- Switzerland Swiss cheese or Cheddar
- Thin-sliced boiled or baked potatoes (with skin)
- Fried onions
- Tomatoes, onions, and lots of garlic
- Bacon bits or diced ham
- Fried tomatoes and green pepper
- Potatoes, sharp cheese, and onions

Toast

A great way to use up stale bread deliciously is to cut it into tiny cubes, fry 'em in butter until brown, then spoon onto half an omelet. For variety, experiment with seasonings: oregano, parsley, curry, garlic, paprika. Sprinkle the seasoning or a combination over the bread as it fries.

Vegetables

Besides onions, three other vegtables are especially good in breakfast or brunch omelets: spinach, mushrooms, and potatoes.

Try a combination of spinach and Greek feta cheese. Or just add a sprinkling of Parmesan or Romano.

Sautéed thin-sliced mushrooms (feel free to use canned) are so flavorful they can solo as filling. In my house, they do.

Any kind of leftover potato (baked, hash-browned, French fried, boiled) can be thin-sliced for filling. Mix with ham or bacon bits. Squirt on the ketchup if that's your thing.

(*see individual vegetable listings*)

6.

Omelets for Lunch and Dinner

When you get into heartier fillings—vegetables, meat, chicken, and fish—you can put omelets on the lunch or dinner menu with a salad or a salad and vegetables, depending on whether it's noon or night. Count on easy cooking whether you're whipping up a meal for 1 or 21.

You also may have the best buy in town because omelets just naturally accommodate bits and pieces of leftovers—a breast of chicken, a lone chop, meat on the bone, a burger patty. What a bargain when you re-cycle leftover odds and ends into a meal.

Don't have too much of any one leftover left over? Combine them or, better yet, offer guests a selection of fillings. They'll find it as much fun as making a choice at Baskin-Robbins.

I've often boasted I could cook omelets from A to Z. It's not exactly the case, although I've come close. I've never made one starting with Q—mainly because leftover quail isn't something you're likely to find in my fridge. And I'm stumped by X. So, from A to Z (minus Q and X), here's how to spark omelets for lunch and dinner.

Asparagus

When asparagus is in season, cook briefly in a small amount of boiling water until just crisp. Fine-chop the tender head of the stalk for omelet filling. Serve the rest of the stalks, cut into 2-inch pieces, to round out the menu.

Avocado

Place thin slices of avocado and tomato on half an omelet. Top with alfalfa sprouts. Fold the omelet, then top with plain yogurt and chopped walnuts.

Beef

You can fry up cubes of leftover beef with potatoes and onions for a hashlike omelet filling. But don't forget that beef combines well with many leftovers. I like to thin-slice it, then add it to the omelet with a tablespoon or two of mashed potatoes (the instant variety will do nicely if you lack leftovers to dip into).

Then there's beef with just about anything that might be hanging out in your fridge, including carrots and peas, a spoonful of ratatouille, tomato and cheese, a crumble of bacon, or some cheesed-up noodles.

Broccoli

For vegetarians who eat eggs, my Supreme Broccoli Omelet is just that. For 4 omelets, I cook a package of frozen broccoli, drain it well, then mix in a small package of cream cheese cut into cubes. A sprinkling of seasoned salt does the rest. Just keep stirring until the cheese melts, then spread on your omelet.

Another combo that's good: sliced broccoli flowerets, cooked mushrooms, and canned peeled tomatoes with a dash of garlic powder, lemon juice, and basil.

Carrots

Remember when Mom mashed carrots and potatoes together for you? It's also great in omelets.

Grated carrot can solo or be used in combination with peas, cheese, bacon bits, pimiento, or green pepper.

Cheese

It's not just because it's alliterative but because it's good that I like shredded Cheddar and chopped chives in an omelet. Also Cheddar and diced bacon.

(*see Cheese, page 40*)

Chicken

Creamed chicken is an omelet filling with expandable virtues. You can add to a little creamed chicken a lot of leftover vegetables—carrots and peas, string beans and mushrooms, potatoes and onions, thin-sliced asparagus, or other combinations of the above.

If you don't have any creamed chicken handy, make the instant kind, adding chopped chicken to warmed undiluted canned cream of celery or mushroom soup.

Leftover sliced chicken combines well with ham, bacon, Switzerland Swiss cheese or fruit.

(*see Turkey, page 57*)

Clams

If you like clams, you'll love them in omelets. When I really feel fancy I make clam fritters, then fine-chop them as omelet filling.

Corned Beef

For a real taste thrill, make a Reuben omelet. Add 1 tablespoon caraway seeds to the egg mixture, then fill the omelet with 2 or 3 thin slices of corned beef, 1 heaping tablespoon of well-drained sauerkraut, 2 to 3 tablespoons of shredded Switzerland Swiss cheese—and, if you want to top it off in a big way, add ¼ cup cooked, crumbled sausage. This goes Reuben a step better.

Crab

Crab, lobster, shrimp! You can afford to serve them in omelets because eggs are always cheap, and remember, a little filling goes a long way. Drizzle with melted butter, hot sauce, hollandaise, mayonnaise. Or cream them and extend with a select vegetable or two.

(see Lobster, page 52)

Dandelions

Dandelion greens cook up like all greens—quickly, in a minimum of water. Drain well, season with lemon juice, and use for an omelet filling that has a nice touch of tartness.

Eggplant

Fried eggplant with its meaty taste makes a hearty filling. Even better, if you happen to have some leftover moussaka around, mush it up and spread on an omelet.

Fish

Leftover fish shouldn't be a total loss. Package it in an omelet but give it pizzazz. Mix it with mayonnaise, tartar sauce, relish, mustard sauce, or tomato sauce. How can you miss?

Frankfurters

(*see Wieners, page 59*)

Gravy

If you've got gravy—canned or leftover—you've got the beginnings of a great omelet filling. Toss in whatever else is hanging out in the leftover file, from a medley of veggies to odds and ends of meat.

Ham

One of the great reasons to bake a Virginia ham is to have leftovers to slice and sandwich into an omelet with mashed sweet potatoes.

(*also see Jelly, page 52; Ham, page 41*)

Herbs

If all else fails, there are herbs. Sprinkle your favorite—basil, thyme, oregano, or parsley flakes—over an omelet. It's not exactly filling but it's flavorful.

Jelly

For lunch or dinner, use jelly with meat. Try mint jelly with lamb; apricot with ham.

(*also see Jam, page 41*)

Kidney Beans

Keep a can of kidney beans on the pantry shelf and you'll never starve to death. They make salads heartier and turn an omelet into a filling meal.

Kippered Herring

A few slices of kippered herring and a squirt of lemon juice go great in an omelet.

Liver

The best bet of all is liver and bacon. Two other combos: liver with peas and mushrooms; liver with tomatoes and onion.

When I feel like an omelet that's like food mother used to make, I sauté chicken livers in butter, then mix them with sour cream and spread them on an omelet with a topping of chopped raw onion.

Lobster

If there's a Chinese fast-food place in your neighborhood, order Lobster Cantonese and save some for an omelet. You'll be glad you did. Creamed lobster's also great in an omelet.

(*see Crab, page 50*)

Macaroni

Gourmets may turn up their nose at this suggestion but one of my favorite omelet fillings comes right out of a can. It's macaroni in creamy cheese sauce, and I really load it on. What a Dagwoodian delight! Any reheated leftover macaroni and cheese, especially with sliced cooked hot dogs, goes over big with the kids.

Mushrooms

Sautéed thin-sliced mushrooms are all the filling an omelet needs. But go on to bigger and better things. Combine mushrooms with other vegetables like peas, scallions, artichoke hearts, asparagus tips, tomatoes, string beans, rice, spaghetti, or a combination of one or more.

P.S. You can use mushrooms in combination with almost every filling in this chapter.

Noodles

Cooked noodles mixed with onion, butter, and Parmesan cheese will give you an omelet filling and a pasta fix.

Olives

Instead of putting olives in your martini, mix them with bacon or cheese (cream or Cheddar).

Onions

French-fried onion rings are one way to fill an omelet. Creamed or fried onions are two traditional others.
(see Onions, page 41)

Oysters

When oysters are in season, try creamed oysters in your omelet. Also oyster fritters.

Potatoes

French fries and shredded cheese—the heat of the omelet will melt the cheese—make an unbeatable combination. It's a personal favorite of mine. Also try mashed potatoes buttered up and mixed with chopped chives or onions.
(see Vegetables, page 44)

Rice

A little rice goes a long way toward filling an omelet when mixed with tomato, peas, mushrooms, or cheese.
(see Wild Rice, page 59)

Salmon

What do you get when you mix flaked canned salmon with chopped celery, onion, dill, and mayonnaise? Salmon-salad omelet filling. You'll be surprised.

Another way to go: Moisten salmon and peas with cream of mushroom soup.

Sandwich

A fun way to serve an omelet: Sandwich it between bread. Bonus: No knife or fork to wash.

Sauerkraut

(*see Corned Beef, page 49*)

Shrimp

(*see Crab, page 50*)

Spinach

Sauté spinach with onions, then fill your omelet, sprinkling grated Switzerland Swiss cheese over the top. Add some raw chopped spinach to the egg batter, too.

(*see Vegetables, page 44*)

Sweetbreads

"The most famous omelettes in the world" are made at Mme. Romaine de Lyon's New York restaurant. The menu lists more than 500 variations on the omelet theme (Mme. Lyon spells it with two t's: omelette) and, of course, sweetbreads, a delicacy popular in France, are included. Mme. Romaine prepares them with peas, onions, croutons, and cheese; mushrooms, croutons, fines herbes, and cheese; spinach, rice, mushrooms, and croutons. Sweetbreads are a treat and you need do nothing more complicated than sauté them briefly in butter until done, slice them, and spoon into your omelet solo or in combinations as suggested here.

Sweetbreads are one of those foods you either like or don't. If you do, a trip to Mme. de Lyons will give you an idea of the many ways you can enjoy them in an omelet.

Tuna

Tuna salad with carrots, peas, and string beans is one of my favorites. If there's a boiled potato around, I might cube it and toss it in.

No leftover veggies? Try tuna salad with sliced pimiento-stuffed olives.

(*see Salmon, page 56*)

Turkey

What could be better than sliced turkey with cranberry relish or giblet gravy or both?

Instead of a sandwich, you also can thin-slice turkey, spread it with mayonnaise, and sandwich it into an omelet.

Or chop the turkey, spread it on half the omelet, and top with ¼ cup shredded cheese.

Or moisten the turkey with a little hot gravy and add some leftover stuffing or mashed potatoes and peas.

Or go gourmet and combine chopped turkey and broccoli in hollandaise. Great for a party!

(*see Chicken, page 49*)

Unfilled

The unfilled omelet isn't an unfulfilled omelet because it can still offer an unexpected taste treat. The surprise isn't in the filling but in the ingredients that are mixed with the eggs. For example:

- Finely chopped onion fried in butter with a dash of paprika
- Chopped asparagus tips
- Diced bacon
- Chopped fines herbes
- Fine-chopped mushrooms—the canned button variety will do very well
- Puréed carrots
- Vegetable mixtures, such as 3 tablespoons of chopped celery, onion and peas or carrots, peas and mushrooms
- Herb mixtures, such as parsley, tarragon, chives, and chervil

Vegetables

If you're dieting, veggies are where it's at. So are omelets.

Knock off the butter and use your nonstick pan as is. You're already saving calories. Flavor the egg mix with ¼ teaspoon dried dill, crushed basil, thyme or oregano for zero calories and lots of flavor. Now live it up and add ⅓ to ½ cup leftover cooked vegetables to half the omelet as filling. This is my Weight Watcher's special.

(see individual vegetable listings)

Wieners

Some things just naturally go with wieners, or franks as nonfood mavens call 'em. Among them: mustard, sauerkraut, and melted cheese. A wiener omelet is almost as popular with kids as one filled with PB & J.

(see Macaroni, page 53)

Wild Rice

Wild rice isn't rice at all. It's grass, but who would look for it listed under "G" except for "Gourmet" or for the "Good" things of life, which foodwise it certainly is. When it's left over from a stuffing or side dish, please consider it for an omelet. I've never used a finer filling.

Yogurt

Because unflavored yogurt can be flavored with your favorite spice (curry, dill, saffron), it'll fill an omelet when there's nothing else around that will.

Zucchini

If you want to take the time, French-fried zucchini is a superb omelet filling. So's zucchini with peeled, chopped tomatoes. Or zucchini dipped in egg, then Parmesan cheese, and fried al dente.

7.

Omelets with an International Flavor

Whoever thought I'd wind up cooking in 20 languages? Not my mother! Little did she know her boy had unsuspected talents and would learn to do more than open and shut the refrigerator door in search of a nosh.

Becoming the world's fastest omelet-maker went to my head. It wasn't enough. I had to become an omelet-maker with an impressive repertoire.

When I'd run the gamut of omelets A to Z (apples to zucchini), I looked for more new worlds to conquer and went ethnic. What could be easier? What's ethnic except a combination of ingredients that appeals to one foreign-speaking group or another?

But ethnic is also impressive. And impressive is what I like to be when I entertain. So while I serve omelets for each and every occasion, my guests never know what may be in store or what language I'm cooking in.

Some of my favorites:

British

Fish and chips make a good omelet filling, but kidneys and gravy more likely are what they serve at Buckingham Palace.

Chinese

You only have to look at a Chinese menu to realize the omelet possibilities are endless because all those stir-fried combos make super fillings. The easiest omelet-making solution: Ask for a doggie bag.

Barring that, whip up your own, trying the choices from my own Column A and Column B:

- Pea pods and canned Chinese vegetables with soy sauce and ginger
- Fried rice with green pepper, green onions, and soy sauce
- Canned chop suey or chow mein
- A garden-fresh stir-fried medley of spinach, mushrooms, bean sprouts, green onions, ginger, and soy sauce. Thicken with a little cornstarch.

French

Everyone has his favorite French restaurant and favorite French omelet. My hit parade:

An omelet filling inspired by onion soup: sautéed onion rings, croutons, and Parmesan cheese.

The ultimate très chic filling: pâté de foie gras and truffles. *Mon dieu! Fantastique!*

The peasant omelet: A ratatouille medley of sautéed vegetables that must feature onion, tomato, and eggplant with whatever else is in season, like green beans or peppers. Sprinkle with basil.

German

Think hot. Think hearty. Think pork and sauerkraut or wieners and sauerkraut. Add a few caraway seeds. Or how about sausage and applesauce. Know what's great? Leftover pot roast and red cabbage with gravy.

Greek

Steal the filling from pasticcio, the Greek answer to lasagna:

Brown onion and chopped beef. Add tomato sauce. When it cooks down, add the barest dash of cinnamon. The Greek word for this is "thavma" (a miracle).

Hawaiian

When you mix crushed pineapple and macadamia nuts, you've got one hula of an omelet. Great for dessert. Even greater with whipped cream topping sprinkled with more crushed macadamias.

Hungarian

It doesn't matter what you put into an omelet. If you flavor it with paprika, it's Hungarian. Leftover goulash is great. Include the noodles.

Indian

Add a dash of curry to the egg mix—a light dash, a medium dash, or be heavy-handed about it if you want to curry flavor in a big way. Fill the omelet with chicken or turkey, chutney and chopped nuts. Shredded coconut and white raisins fit too.

Irish

On March 18, the omelet filling to make features the March 17 leftovers: corned beef and cabbage.

Potato, onion, and bacon add up to another combination that smacks of the auld sod, making as fine a breakfast as a man could want.

And don't forget that superb Irish smoked salmon. It's a treat.

Italian

Let an omelet be the "crust" for a pizza dish. Add a pinch of garlic powder and oregano to the egg mix, then spread the omelet with pizza sauce, shredded mozzarella cheese, and, if desired, any or all of the following: pepperoni, hot sausage, mushrooms.

Another Italian mixture: zucchini, onions, and cheese with oregano and basil.

Japanese

Now that you can find Japanese-style vegetables in the frozen-food department, you know what to do: Cook 'em up for an omelet filling. Add shrimp, tuna, or crabmeat chunks.

Jewish

What do you get when you top slices of lox with sour cream? A Jewish omelet filling. Make sure everyone gets the message by serving it with hot toasted bagels.

Mexican

Chili up an omelet and, caramba! it's Mexican.

Try:

Chili with corn, tomato, zucchini, a splash of taco sauce, and a little cumin—a super spice with lots of punch.

Chopped beef, chili, canned peeled tomatoes or tomato sauce, chopped onion, and pimiento.

Kidney beans and anything.

Serve an omelet on a tortilla, especially an omelet filled with green chilies, onion, and tomato sauce.

Middle Eastern

Everyone lays claim to the eggplant, a Middle Eastern favorite. Simmered with onion and tomatoes in olive oil until mushy, it's marvelous.

Portuguese Omelet

Place canned sardines on an omelet and drizzle on tomato sauce.

Russian

This one's so classy, it's fit for a commissar: Spread your omelet with red or black caviar, then add dollops of divinely sour cream.

Scandinavian

The health-conscious Scandinavians combine vegetables, fruit, and bacon in omelets—like onion, potatoes, bacon, prunes and apples. Great when they're all sautéed together in butter.

South American

South of the border, people by the bunch love banana omelets. So simple:

Sauté in butter, then add plantain chips for a nice touch of crunch. Sprinkle on some ground cloves or allspice and grated orange rind.

Spanish

The price of saffron being what it is, you can consider a saffron omelet deluxe party fare.

Economize and add just a pinch to the egg mixture

for color. Splurge and use it to flavor a filling of shrimp or chicken and peeled tomatoes with rice. Toss in some Spanish olives or sautéed green pepper.

Leftover paella with its medley of flavors is perfect in an omelet—but then, what isn't?

Swiss

With all those cheeses for which Switzerland is so justly famous, it's small wonder that the Swiss cheese up their omelets. Who can blame them?

I like their grated Gruyère with sherry and dry mustard.

Even better is an omelet filled with raclette, a cheese that's sliced, heated in the oven, and served marvelously melted.

Do I have to tell you what to do with leftover fondue? Problem is, there's so seldom any left over.

8.

The Grand Finale:
Dessert Omelets

If I knew you were coming would I bake a cake? Not likely, though I might buy one because I'm lazy. For that very reason I often whip up a dessert omelet.

Contrary to what you might suppose, I don't serve omelets as the main course and then omelets for dessert, although I've been tempted. Still, leave them asking for more is a good rule in show biz—and in the kitchen.

Dessert omelets, like all omelets, are a whiz to whip up. They'll never leave you at a loss for it's guaranteed there is something in your kitchen cupboard or refrigerator that can turn 2 eggs and 2 tablespoons water into a grand finale.

For example, almost any kind of fruit makes an instant omelet dessert. For a real rich touch, mix sour cream or whipped cream with fruit, even some chopped nuts or shredded coconut, and you've got a sundae-best treat.

Among my favorite dessert fillings:

Apples

Sauté a sliced apple in butter, then sprinkle with brown sugar, a dash of cinnamon or nutmeg.

Or how about apple-pie filling sparked with some shredded Cheddar? This one's wonderful.

Apricot

Fresh or canned sliced apricots go into the omelet and apricot brandy and powdered sugar are drizzled over the outside of the omelet—you can't miss. The brandy mixes with the sugar in the hot pan and turns thick and syrupy.

Bananas

Don't put bananas in the refrigerator if you're going to put them in an omelet. They shouldn't be cold. Room temperature's O.K. Warm is even better.

Something super happens when you sauté sliced bananas briefly in a little butter. It brings out the flavor. So sauté away, then spread the thin-sliced bananas on half of your omelet and sprinkle with walnuts, pecans, almonds, and maybe some flaked coconut.

Know what else is good? Bananas and brown sugar. Also bananas and yogurt with a topping of wheat germ or cereal flakes. Or borrow New Orleans' famous Bananas Foster topping for ice cream (hot bananas, brown sugar, nuts and rum) to make an omelet filling.

(*see South American, page 68*)

Cherries

Seeding cherries to put them into an omelet is the pits, so use cherry-pie filling instead. Or frozen whole cherries. Mush them up with cream cheese, sour cream, or whipped cream. It's so good you'll finally understand why little George Washington chopped down that cherry tree. Certainly, he was going to make a cherry omelet.

Cherry-pie filling and a spoonful of Cherry Heering are a good combination too.

Cranberries

Don't worry if you forget to serve the cranberry sauce or relish with the Thanksgiving turkey. Just stash it away and use it to make a dessert omelet. I like cranberry filling with whipped cream, nuts, and a good dusting of confectioners sugar.

Jam and Jelly

Never say die—or diet—when you're toying with the idea of dessert. You may think there's nothing around to toss into a dessert omelet but there always is —like jam or jelly. Pick your favorite flavor and spread away. If you must keep an eye on calories, reduced-sugar preserves offer a lower-calorie way to enjoy a sweet treat. At only 160 calories per 2 eggs you can splurge on the filling.

Mincemeat

Why is it we seldom think of mincemeat until it's turkey time? It's delicious, especially in an omelet. Spark it with brandy. Add some chopped walnuts for crunch. Va-va-va-VOOM!

Nectarines

Try sliced nectarines, sprinkled with brown sugar and finely chopped dried apricots.

Oranges

If you want to go all out orange for an omelet, add a little grated orange rind to the egg mix and spread the omelet with chopped oranges, grated coconut, and a few drops of orange liqueur. Serve your omelet garnished with orange slices and whipped cream. I use lots of whipped cream now that it squirts out of pres-

surized cans and I don't have to wear myself out whipping it into a frenzy of peaks.

Chopped oranges and bananas make a nice filling, too.

Use canned mandarin oranges when you don't have time to spend peeling. Use fresh California navals when they're in season. But do use oranges!

Peaches

Peaches and cream describe complexions—they also describe a superb omelet filling.

Even better, stew peaches in a little water with sugar and brandy. Spread the well-drained result in your omelet and the thickened liquid on top.

Or try peaches and puréed strawberries.

Peanut Butter

I know a peanut-butter omelet is dessert when I jazz it up with goodies like chopped dates, slivered or chopped almonds, walnuts, pecans, or—would you believe—peanuts? I like crunchiness. And don't forget PB and raisins, maraschino cherries, flaked coconut, or macaroon crumbs. Really flip out and mix PB with chocolate or butterscotch chips.

Do I have to suggest peanut-butter combos to PB aficionados? I doubt it.

(*see Peanut Butter, page 43*)

Pears

Canned Bartlett pears were made with omelet filling in mind. Juicy fresh Bartletts are good, too. Try them with shredded Cheddar cheese and you'll know the true meaning of an old Italian proverb that says, "Never tell the peasants how good is a pear with cheese."

Another way to make pear filling is to simmer diced pears with sugar, butter, nutmeg, and rum until the butter melts. Don't taste too much while cooking or you'll be shy on omelet filling.

Pineapples

Remember that sandwich you used to take to school in a brown paper bag—or maybe you had a lunch box? Well, pineapple tidbits mashed into cream cheese make more than a sandwich. They make a superb omelet filling.

Try pineapple tidbits mixed with puréed strawberries, too. Or pineapple tidbits, chopped mandarin oranges, honey, and cinnamon.

For a doubly good treat, combine pineapple preserves or crushed pineapple and pineapple yogurt.

Raisins

Raisins and just about any fruit can add up to dessert omelet. If there's nothing else around that says "dessert," let raisins solo.

Strawberries

Strawberries go with everything—whipped cream (wow!), sour cream (yum!), cream cheese (now you're talking!). Choose your favorite. Mine is puréed strawberries whipped into cream cheese. You could spread a layer of thin-sliced bananas over this. Or you could be a purist and enjoy it as is.

Then there's strawberries and pineapple or just plain puréed strawberries and sugar.

Anthony May, co-owner of New York City's Rainbow Room, soaks sliced strawberries in Marsala wine for about an hour and a half before folding an omelet around them. Then he cuts slits on top, drops in some cinnamon and brown sugar, then runs it under the broiler just until it's caramelized. Be sure you use a pan with an ovenproof handle (or use any pan with the handle covered completely with two layers of aluminum foil).

I like strawberries.

Disappointed that I missed your favorite fruit—kiwi, blueberries, mango, rhubarb, grapes? Or that maybe I overlooked your favorite omelet dessert filling (chocolate, butterscotch, maple)? If I did, improvise. That's the fun of omelet-making. It's as creative as you are.

THE FLAMING OMELET

The most impressive dessert of all is the flaming omelet. Lower the house lights, raise your match, and flambé away before the admiring eyes of everyone in the room.

While you can whip up omelets infinitum in the kitchen, the instant you put a match to an omelet, go public. This is a big number and people will be impressed.

Omelet Flambé

Here's what you do:

Bring the filled omelet in the hot pan to the table. Dust with about a tablespoon of confectioners sugar. Pour about 3 tablespoons of 70-proof fruit-flavored brandy over the top of the omelet, then quickly ignite it with a long (fireplace) match, tilting the pan so all the brandy will burn. Baste as the brandy flames, then spoon the omelet out straight from the pan topped with a dollop of sour cream or whipped cream. One omelet will serve four absolutely dazzled people.

Important: If you use a liquor that's more than 70 proof, use less—unless you have an 18-foot ceiling!

LEFTOVERS MAKE DESSERTS, TOO

The omelet not only is a catchall for leftovers that turn it into a main dish, but a catchall for leftovers that turn it into an entirely different dessert.

Stale cake? Soak it in a sweet liqueur, or mash in some fresh fruit and use as filling. Trust me.

A wedge of pie? Discard the crust and spoon the pie filling into the omelet.

Fresh or canned fruit salad? Spark with whipped cream and spread on your omelet.

You should have the message by now. When it comes to omelets, anything and everything goes. It's up to you.

9.

Omelets by Any Other Name

When I found my place in the Culinary Hall of Fame —in a kitchen niche next to an omelet pan—I knew I'd arrived and was content to stay put. I'd achieved my goal and could stave off starvation in 40 seconds flat with a showy measure of savoir flair.

But what of you? Not everyone wants to keep his status quo. Spurred on by success, you may feel ready to muscle in on James Beard, Jacques Pepin, Julia Child, and other culinary giants whose expertise is far more than a flash in the omelet pan.

If try you must, stick with what you know—omelets, and master some of the more intricate and sophisticated dishes in this category. The truth is that the omelet is well-connected and has close relations in the haute cuisine. I never said they were easy to make but if, like those who scale Mt. Everest, you like a challenge, it's time to move on to omelets by any other name. They include:

WESTERN/DENVER OMELET

A Western (or Denver) omelet is simply scrambled eggs with lots of filling "stuff"—traditionally, diced green peppers, onions, and ham (I use kosher salami) that's sautéed in butter right in the omelet pan. The beaten egg is poured over it all and the omelet is made with no further regard for filling or folding. When it's done, flip it over if you like or just slide it out of the pan onto a plate. Or make a sandwich of it. Use as much "stuff" as you like. There's no hard-and-fast recipe to follow.

Just because the peppers, onions, and ham are imprisoned in the egg doesn't mean you can't give this all-American omelet a French touch by filling and folding it anyhow. I use sharp Cheddar cheese as a filling. Then it's no longer exactly a Western omelet, but it's better, so who cares?

HANGTOWN FRY

The prospectors who cooked over camp fires in Gold Rush days hit a mother lode when they dreamed up an omelet with bacon and oysters. There are dozens of versions and variations. Here's my favorite.

4 thick slices bacon
1 tablespoon butter
8 large oysters
Flour
4 eggs
4 tablespoons milk or cream
Salt and pepper
Lemon juice

SERVES 4

For 1 omelet, fry bacon slices in the omelet pan until crisp. Remove from pan and reserve. Pour off all but about a tablespoon of fat from the pan and add butter. Dust oysters with flour and sauté in the butter and fat. Meanwhile, beat eggs with milk or cream plus salt and pepper to taste. Crumble the bacon and add to the egg mixture.

When the oysters are golden brown, pour the egg mixture on top and make a Western/Denver-style omelet.

Cut into quarters and serve with a little fresh lemon juice squirted on top.

83

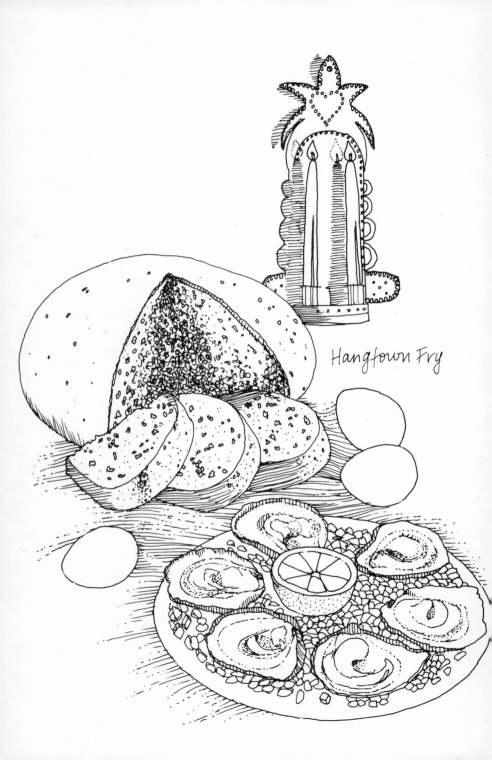

Hangtown Fry

Northern Californians often eat their Hangtown Fry in a buttered sourdough roll. Mmmm.

TORTILLA-STYLE OMELET

Some recipes call this type of omelet a "tortilla," although the tortillas I know and love are made with cornmeal. This isn't, but it gets chewy and the consistency is somewhat tortillalike. It's simply an omelet for 4 done Western/Denver style (the filling is cooked right in with the egg mixture until the egg is set). The whole round "pancake" is then inverted and cooked some more. It's served sliced in wedges. Like all other omelets, it may be filled with anything handy.

To serve 4, fry small slices of ham, sliced potatoes, diced green and red peppers, and diced onion until crisp. Pour 8 eggs mixed with 8 tablespoons of water over the sautéed vegetables. Sprinkle shredded Cheddar cheese on top and let the egg cook—untouched—until set, or until the cheese melts and blends in. Turn the whole thing over by sliding it onto a lightly buttered plate. Invert the plate over the pan so the omelet lands back in the pan upside down. Continue to cook to desired doneness. Slide back onto the plate and cut into 4 wedges.

FRITTATA

A frittata, the omelet's Italian connection, is essentially a Western omelet that's cooked on both sides, then the top is finished in the broiler. It's Italian not because of what's in it, but where it originated, so don't think for a moment that it needs to contain things Italian. I especially love this spinach frittata. But, as for all omelets, fillings for a frittata are as limitless as your imagination—or what you've got on hand in the kitchen.

A beautiful open-face omelet that serves 4, you can cut this into wedges and serve it right from the pan.

SPINACH FRITTATA

> 1 10-ounce package frozen chopped spinach
> ½ pound fresh mushrooms, sliced, or
>   1 4-ounce can sliced mushrooms (see Notes)
> ¼ cup finely chopped onion or 1 tablespoon
>   instant minced onion
> 3 tablespoons butter
> 8 eggs
> ½ teaspoon seasoned salt
> Dash pepper
> ⅓ cup grated Parmesan cheese
> Parsley and red peppers (optional)

SERVES 4

Cook spinach according to package directions. Drain well, pressing out excess liquid.

Meanwhile, in a large ovenproof frying pan (see Notes) cook mushrooms and onions in butter over medium heat until tender but not brown, 7 to 10 minutes. Beat together eggs, salt, and pepper. Stir in drained spinach. Pour over mushrooms and onions. Cook over low to medium heat until eggs are set, about 7 minutes.

Sprinkle with cheese, broil about 6 inches from heat until cheese melts, 2 to 3 minutes. Cut into wedges to serve. Garnish with parsley and peppers, if desired.

Notes: If using canned mushrooms and instant minced onion, do not sauté in butter. Add mushrooms with liquid and instant minced onion to egg mixture. Cook as above.

To make handle ovenproof, cover completely with 2 layers of aluminum foil.

PUFFY OMELET

To my way of thinking, if you're going to go through the hassle of separating eggs, beating whites stiff, folding in yolks, turning on the oven, and trying to borrow a pan with a heatproof handle from a neighbor, you'd be smarter to go a step or two further and make a gloriously grand soufflé instead of a puffy omelet. But that's your business. A puffy omelet makes a beautiful presentation but a soufflé is a show-stopper. Since this book is about omelets, not soufflés, here's the recipe for:

BASIC PUFFY OMELET

4 eggs, separated
¼ cup water
¼ teaspoon salt
¼ teaspoon cream of tartar
1 tablespoon butter

SERVES 2

Beat egg whites with water, salt, and cream of tartar at high speed until stiff but not dry, or just until whites no longer slip when bowl is tilted. Beat egg yolks at high speed until thick and lemon colored, about 5 minutes. Fold yolks into whites.

Heat butter in 10-inch omelet pan or frying pan with ovenproof handle over medium-high heat until just hot enough to sizzle a drop of water. Pour in omelet mixture and gently smoothe surface. Reduce heat to medium. Cook slowly until puffy and lightly browned on bottom, about 5 minutes. Lift omelet at edge to judge color. Bake in preheated 350° F oven 10 to 12 minutes, or until knife inserted halfway between center and outside edge comes out clean.

To serve, loosen omelet edges with a spatula. With a sharp knife cut the upper surface down the center of omelet but *do not* cut through to the bottom of the omelet. Fill with any filling you like as with any omelet. With pancake turner, fold in half and turn out onto a plate with a quick flip of the wrist. Serve immediately.

OMELET "TORTE"

Make *two* puffy omelets in succession (just double the Puffy Omelet recipe). When the first omelet comes out of the oven, slide it out of the pan onto a warm plate and set it aside while the second omelet is prepared. Place a generous amount of filling (ham, cheese, mushrooms, peppers, asparagus, bacon, whatever) on top of the first omelet. Take the second omelet from the oven and invert the pan over the first so the omelet lands upside down on the filling. Pour a sauce appropriate to the filling over the entire "torte." Sprinkle on some more filling. To serve, cut into wedges.

This torte is a superb dessert filled with fruit and topped with a sweet sauce.

OMELET PUFFS (Puffy Omelet Hors d'oeuvres)

Preheat your oven to 425° F. Prepare a Puffy Omelet mixture. Instead of pouring it into the buttered pan all at once, spoon the mixture, a heaping teaspoonful at a time, into the pan and cook until the under side is brown (you can get about 8 dollops to a batch in a 10-inch omelet pan). Transfer the dollops to a greased cookie sheet and continue making batches this way. Before baking, sprinkle each dollop with any kind of shredded cheese and a dash of your favorite herb. Bake for 5 minutes.

You can really flavor up these puffs with minced clams, deviled ham, pepperoni, shredded salami, bacon bits, olives, etc. Like any omelet filling, sky-high's the limit.

ROULADE (Puffy Omelet Roll)

Roulade is a great, big beautiful sponge that's known as the "jelly roll" of the omelet family. It rolls around filling like sponge cake rolls around jelly and looks so spectacular when served, I don't even mind cutting it into 6 serving portions. Lots of steps are involved but if, like me, you don't mind hassling around the kitchen to whip up a soufflé for 4 or 6, you'll take them in stride. A spectacular is a spectacular and that's what Roulade is.

Choose and use your favorite filling to make it lunch, brunch, dinner, or dessert. Serve 1-slice portions for an appetizer or dieter's dessert; 2 slices for an entrée.

4 eggs, separated
¼ teaspoon cream of tartar
¼ teaspoon salt
⅓ cup all-purpose flour
Filling, as preferred
Sauce, as preferred
¼ cup melted butter

SERVES 4 TO 6

Lightly grease a 15½ x 10½ x 1-inch jelly-roll pan. Line bottom with waxed paper. Grease again.

In large mixing bowl, beat egg whites, cream of tartar, and salt at high speed until stiff but not dry, just until whites no longer slip when bowl is tilted.

In large mixing bowl, beat egg yolks until thick and lemon colored, about 5 minutes. Sprinkle flour over yolks. Gently fold in beaten whites until thoroughly blended. Pour into prepared pan, spreading batter evenly.

Bake in preheated 400° F oven until top of sponge roll springs back when lightly touched with finger, 8 to 10 minutes.

Loosen sponge roll from sides of pan with spatula and invert onto clean towel which has been covered with waxed paper. Carefully pull waxed paper off bottom of baked sponge roll. Trim all edges. Starting from narrow edge, roll up sponge roll, rolling waked paper in with sponge roll. Wrap in paper towel and place seam side down on wire rack until cool, about 30 minutes.

Meanwhile, prepare your favorite filling and sauce.

Unwrap sponge roll and carefully brush with butter. Spread evenly with filling. Reroll. Cut into 12 slices about ¾ inch thick. Spoon sauce over slices.

FLAT-OUT OMELETS

FLAT OMELET ROLL (Roulade)

This is my own creation. It's an adaptation of the Roulade but requires no soufflé steps. In fact, it's a simple, basic omelet that's rolled and sliced. It requires a 12- to 15-inch skillet (15-inch skillets are electric, square, and ideal for this).

For 4 people, make 1 big omelet with 8 eggs and 8 tablespoons of water. Place the filling all over the top of it. (My favorite filling for this is Switzerland Swiss cheese slices and whole cooked asparagus spears.) Roll the omelet up with your hands and lift it with a spatula onto a serving platter. Slice and serve topped with an appropriate sauce. For asparagus and cheese, it's hollandaise, naturally.

EGG FOO YUNG

The French gave us the omelet as a part of their then-new haute cuisine back in the fifteenth century.

But 600 years before that, the Chinese were cooking Egg Foo Yung, which doesn't exactly translate into the French word "omelette" in anyone's Berlitz book. Still, the concept is the same. The shape is different.

In the interest of saving time and effort (which are the next best things to saving money), this version uses canned Oriental vegetables. They work out fine but you don't need your mother to tell you the fresh is better—always. Not quicker—but better. So now that bean sprouts, water chestnuts, bamboo shoots, snow peas, and other Oriental produce have escaped big-city Chinatowns and are available lots of places, give them a try.

EGG FOO YUNG CANTONESE

3 tablespoons butter
1 16-ounce can bean sprouts, drained
1 16-ounce can Chinese mixed vegetables,
*   drained*
¾ cup chopped onions
¾ cup chopped celery
2 tablespoons chopped green pepper
8 eggs, slightly beaten
2 teaspoons soy sauce (3 teaspoons if using
*   fresh vegetables)*
Oil (enough to cover depth of pan ½ inch)
       8 TO 10 PANCAKES (2 PER SERVING)

Melt butter. Add all vegetables and cook over medium heat until onions are soft. Allow to cool. In a large mixing bowl, mix eggs with soy sauce. Add vegetables.

Heat oil to moderately hot. Drop in egg mixture to form 4- or 5-inch pancakes. Cook until brown, about 4 minutes on each side. Drain on paper towel. Serve with rice and Cantonese Sauce.

ORIENTAL EGG SKINS

This is one of the more obscure omelets. It's so easy, unique, and delicious, I don't know why it never caught on. It is an omelet that is really a soft casing for all sorts of Oriental fillings. I'm told that it's Vietnamese in origin. It's like a crepe or blintz but forms a bundle instead of a roll with an Oriental sort of filling inside. Egg skins can be made well in advance of serving, then filled and fried in a little oil before bringing to the table.

To simplify preparation, I use frozen or canned Oriental fillings such as assorted Chinese or Japanese vegetables, frozen or canned fried rice, chow mein, chop suey, sweet and sour pork, etc. Or, whatever is left over from my last visit to a Chinese restaurant.

For 4 servings, combine 1 tablespoon cornstarch with 1 tablespoon water. Beat into 4 eggs. Remove 1 tablespoon of this mixture and set aside to seal the bundles later.

Pour ¼ of the mixture into a lightly oiled, hot, 10-inch omelet pan, twirling the pan quickly as you pour to fully coat the bottom. Cook 1 to 2 minutes until the top is dry and the bottom is lightly browned. Slide onto waxed paper. Make 3 more such pancakes.

You'll need about 3 cups of filling. Spoon ¼ of the filling (about ¾ cup) across and just below the center of one omelet, leaving approximately 1-inch margins on the sides. Press the filling together gently but firmly. Fold in the side margins, then the bottom and top to make an envelope-type bundle. Seal the edges of the omelet with a little of the reserved egg mixture. Repeat this three more times.

When ready to serve, fry omelets seam side down in a small amount of hot oil until golden. Turn and brown on the other side. Serve with soy sauce.

KAISERSCHMARRN (Emperor's Omelet)

This is a sweet Austrian dessert—and who knows more about dessert than the Austrians? It's somewhat like a tortilla-type omelet but, unlike any other omelet I know, it is served shredded with stewed fruit or compote.

You could have hummed the entire score of "Tales from the Vienna Woods" while the emperor's chef whipped this goodie up. I tried it his way the first time out and then got smart. I simplified preparation by whipping it up in a blender faster than I can whistle the first bar of "Dixie."

> *4 eggs, separated*
> *2 cups milk*
> *1 cup flour*
> *2 tablespoons sugar*
> *Salt*
> *2 tablespoons raisins, or to taste*
> *Cinnamon*

SERVES 6

Put the yolks, milk, flour, sugar, and a pinch of salt into a blender and blend at medium to high speed until smooth. Beat egg whites until stiff and gently fold into batter. Stir in at least 2 tablespoons of raisins.

Pour mixture into a moderately hot, buttered 10- or 12-inch skillet and let it cook, undisturbed, until brown on bottom.

Turn the whole thing over by sliding it onto a lightly buttered plate, then invert the plate over the pan so the omelet lands back in the pan upside down. Continue to cook until the other side browns.

Shred the omelet, using two forks, and spoon out of the pan. Spoon on stewed fruit or compote. Sprinkle each serving with additional sugar and some cinnamon.

MATZO BREI

Before the revolution in Russia, my grandmother learned from her grandmother who learned from her grandmother how to make Matzo Brei. I'm not sure whether this is more like French toasted matzo or a matzo omelet done frittata style. I don't really care because I make it often, and mostly serve it as a side dish instead of potatoes. Or I eat it for breakfast with powdered sugar and preserves.

Matzo is a real serendipity. It was first reported in the Old Testament Book of Exodus. When Moses led the Jews from Egypt, they left so quickly they had no time to wait for their bread dough to rise, so they skipped the leavening process altogether and baked the bread flat. The result was a crisp, thin, crackerlike flat bread called matzo. Today, it's available in supermarkets everywhere. If you've never tried it, do.

GRANDMA'S MATZO BREI

4 eggs
1 cup water
Salt and pepper
6 squares of matzos

SERVES 2

Mix eggs with water, salt, and pepper. Run matzo, a square at a time, under warm running water from the tap. Coarsely crumble matzo into egg mixture. Let soak 5 minutes.

Fry in butter like any omelet in a medium hot pan until dry. Cut in half. If you'd like a little onion flavor, sauté some diced onion into the pan while the matzo is soaking.

10.

The Omelet as Masterpiece:
Hitting the Sauce

For years, I enjoyed hitting the sauce in omelet restaurants but never tried making a sauce at home because I was intimidated. I knew what went into sauces— secret spices and lots of stirring.

Then two wonderful things happened: I got a blender and the recipe for Basic Medium White Sauce. Liberation!

Talk about one thing leading to another. That's what the chef who created Medium White Sauce had in mind. A cooking secret almost as super as the 40-second omelet, it is the basis for 12 of the sauces in this chapter, every one of them calculated to turn an omelet into a major masterpiece.

You'll find ethnic saucery in this chapter, too, because Italian, French, and Chinese sauces are impressively good. I've also included a few of my favorite sweet sauces because they do dreamy things for dessert omelets.

All you have to do with any of these sauces is spoon them over plain or filled omelets. Be sparing or let your omelet swim in sauce, as you prefer. If you like lots of sauce, serve thick slices of toast or bread with breakfast, brunch, lunch, or dinner omelets and dunk right in; with dessert omelets, pass cubes of pound cake—fresh or stale—then spear and swirl 'em in the sauce.

A DOZEN SAUCES HATCH FROM ONE

Master this 1 simple blender sauce and 12 others will fall into your sauce repertoire with no trouble at all. It's the basis of all cream sauces. It emerges from the blender entirely lump-free, and may be kept warm on the top of a double boiler over simmering water. It's wondrous. Note that the variations will call for either the *medium* or *thick* version. The *thick* version is used in recipes that add ingredients that will thin down the sauce.

101

BASIC BLENDER MEDIUM *WHITE SAUCE*

1 cup hot milk
2 tablespoons flour
2 tablespoons soft butter

1 CUP

Measure ingredients in blender or food processor container. Cover and blend on high speed until smooth. Pour into saucepan and cook over low heat for 3 minutes, stirring occasionally. Season to taste with salt and pepper.

BASIC BLENDER THICK *WHITE SAUCE*

1¼ CUPS

Use 3 tablespoons flour and 3 tablespoons soft butter in preparing above recipe.

Cheese Sauce

You can substitute Swiss or Edam, Monterey Jack, Gruyère, or any cheese in this sauce. Good for vegetables, ham, plain, or herb omelet.

Add to blender container, along with other ingredients for Medium White Sauce (see above): ¼ pound sharp Cheddar cheese, diced; ¼ teaspoon dry

mustard, ¼ teaspoon paprika, and a dash of Tabasco. Makes 1¼ cups.

Tomato Sauce

Good for zucchini, cheese, bacon, or herb omelet.

To 1 cup hot Medium White Sauce (see page 102), blend in 6 tablespoons tomato paste. Makes 1–1⅓ cups.

Creole Sauce

Good for ham, mushroom, vegetable, cheese omelet.

To Tomato Sauce (see above), stir in ¼ cup each chopped celery and green pepper, 2 tablespoons minced onion, and a dash of Tabasco. Simmer over low heat for 30 minutes or until vegetables are tender. Makes 2 cups.

Chicken à la King Sauce

Good for plain, herb, spinach omelet. Use as filler or topper.

To 1 cup hot Thick White Sauce (see page 102), stir in ½ cup each heavy cream, diced chicken or turkey, and sautéed mushrooms, 1 canned pimiento, diced; add 1 tablespoon dry sherry. Cook over low heat until heated through. Makes 2½ cups.

Blue Cheese and Olive Sauce

Good for vegetable, bacon, avocado, tomato, ham, chicken, or shrimp omelet.

To 1 cup Medium White Sauce, stir in ½ cup diced ripe black olives, ¼ cup crumbled blue cheese. Makes 1–1¾ cups.

Sauce Béchamel

A French version of Basic White Sauce.

To 1 cup Medium White Sauce, add 2 tablespoons finely minced onion and a pinch each of nutmeg and thyme. Cook over low heat for 30 minutes, stirring occasionally. Makes 1¼ cups.

Velouté Sauce

Substitute 1 cup chicken or fish broth for milk in Sauce Béchamel. A French version of Basic White Sauce.

Curry Sauce

Good for vegetable, seafood, or chicken omelet.

To 1 cup hot Medium Sauce Béchamel, stir in 1 tablespoon each curry powder and lemon juice and 1 clove garlic, crushed. Makes 1 cup.

Florentine Sauce

Good for feta cheese, olive, bacon, herb, vegetable, or plain omelet.

To 1 cup hot Medium Sauce Béchamel, add 1 cup cooked chopped spinach, well drained; ½ teaspoon Worcestershire sauce, and a dash of Tabasco. Cook until heated through. Makes 2 cups.

Mornay Sauce

A French cheese sauce.

To 1 cup thick Sauce Béchamel, add to saucepan 2 tablespoons each diced Gruyère and Parmesan cheese. Cook as directed. Before using, stir in 2 tablespoons of butter bit by bit. Makes 1¼ cups.

Mushroom Sauce

Good for vegetable, bacon, avocado, tomato, ham, chicken, or shrimp omelet.

To 1 cup hot, thick Sauce Béchamel, add ½ cup sautéed mushrooms or 1 4-ounce can mushrooms and juice. Makes 1½ cups.

Newburg Sauce

Good for any seafood omelet.

To 1 cup thick Sauce Béchamel, stir in 1 egg yolk beaten with ¼ cup heavy cream and 2 tablespoons dry sherry. If desired, stir in ½ cup cooked shrimp, crabmeat, or lobster. Makes 1½–2 cups.

MORE ENTRÉE SAUCES

ITALIAN TOMATO SAUCE

This goes very well with a ham, ground meat, sausage, or zucchini omelet.

¼ cup olive oil
1 clove garlic, minced
1 medium onion, minced
1 32-oz. can Italian plum tomatoes
2 tablespoons tomato paste
2 tablespoons dried basil
Salt and pepper
1 tablespoon chopped parsley

3 CUPS

Heat oil in saucepan. Add garlic and onion, cook for 2 to 3 minutes. Add tomatoes and tomato paste. Bring to a boil and simmer, uncovered, for 15 minutes. Add basil and season with salt and pepper to taste. Before serving, sprinkle with parsley.

PESTO SAUCE

One of my favorite Italian sauces. Tastes just as good on plain omelets as it does on pasta.

⅓ *cup olive oil*
¼ *cup grated Parmesan cheese*
¼ *cup chopped parsley*
1 clove garlic, quartered
2 tablespoons basil
1 teaspoon salt
¼ *teaspoon nutmeg*

½ CUP

Measure all ingredients into blender or food processor container. Blend until well mixed.

CANTONESE LOBSTER SAUCE

Good with Egg Foo Yung, seafood, asparagus, Chinese vegetables, mushroom omelets. Don't look for the lobster in this sauce. It got its name because the Chinese often served it with lobster.

¼ cup peanut oil
½ pound lean ground pork
4 scallions, sliced thin
1 stalk celery, sliced fine
1 cup chicken broth
1½ teaspoons salt
1 teaspoon pepper
2 eggs, well beaten

Thickening
2½ tablespoons flour
2 teaspoons soy sauce
¼ cup water

2½ CUPS

Heat oil in frying pan until very hot. Add pork, scallions, and celery. Stir-fry for 1 minute. Slowly add broth, salt, and pepper and bring to a boil. Cover pan, reduce heat and cook 10 minutes.

Mix thickening ingredients together. Add to pan and simmer for 4 minutes. Stir in beaten eggs. Heat 1 minute.

SLOPPY JOE CHILI SAUCE

Use as a filler or topper. Sprinkle with grated Cheddar cheese. If desired, run under the broiler to melt.

½ pound ground beef
1 small onion, chopped
¼ cup chopped green pepper
½ cup bottled barbecue sauce
1 tablespoon chili powder
Salt and pepper to taste

2½ CUPS

Sauté meat, onion, and green pepper in skillet, stirring with a fork to break up meat until meat is lightly browned and vegetables are tender. Add remaining ingredients and simmer, covered, stirring occasionally for 10 minutes.

QUICKIE CHEESE SAUCE

Heat 1 can Cheddar cheese soup, undiluted. Stir in 2 to 3 tablespoons beer, wine, barbecue sauce, or chili sauce, etc., if desired.

Add bacon bits, olives, pimiento, croutons, diced tomatoes. My sons love 2 tablespoons of pickle relish stirred in. Makes 1½ cups.

HOLLANDAISE SAUCE

While this is a French concoction, the name may come from the fact that Holland is famous for its butter, a main constituent of the sauce. Louis Diat, chef extraordinaire and sauce expert formerly with New York City's Ritz Carlton, wrote that "if the sauce does curdle, you can bring it back to homogenous thickness by putting a fresh egg yolk in another pan and gradually whipping in the curdled mixture." The blender method avoids the curdling problem altogether.

> *3 egg yolks*
> *2 tablespoons lemon juice*
> *¼ teaspoon salt*
> *⅛ teaspoon paprika*
> *Dash cayenne pepper*
> *½ cup (1 stick) butter, chilled and cut into*
> * eighths*
>
> ¾ CUP

In saucepan, beat together egg yolks, lemon juice, and seasonings. Add half the butter. Cook over low heat, stirring rapidly, until butter melts. Add remaining butter, stirring constantly, until butter melts and sauce thickens. Cover and refrigerate if not using immediately. Makes ¾ cup.

To Prepare in Blender: Measure all ingredients except butter into blender container. Melt butter and add to other ingredients. Blend at low speed until sauce thickens, 15 to 20 seconds.

MUSTARD SAUCE

Belonging to the sweet-sour family of recipes, this sauce complements a variety of dishes. It is well suited to ham or other pork cuts, as well as many vegetables. A quick spin in the blender assures a smooth texture and constant stirring, while cooking over medium-high heat, gives creamy results.

1 egg
¼ cup water
¼ cup vinegar
2 tablespoons sugar
1½ tablespoons dry mustard
1 tablespoon butter
¼ teaspoon salt
Dash nutmeg

⅔ CUP

Measure all ingredients into blender container or small mixing bowl. Blend or mix at medium speed until well combined. Pour into small saucepan. Cook over medium-high heat, stirring constantly, just until mixture comes to a boil. Remove from heat.

POLONAISE SAUCE

Unlike many sauces in which eggs are used as a thickener, to this one add hard-cooked eggs for color and texture. In the nineteenth century, A. Carême, a famous French chef, published a version of Polonaise that was similar, but included horseradish. This Polonaise is well suited to fish and vegetable omelets.

¼ cup butter
3 tablespoons snipped parsley
1 tablespoon lemon juice
1 ½ teaspoons instant minced onion
Dash salt
Dash pepper
2 tablespoons fine dry bread crumbs
2 hard-cooked egg yolks, finely chopped or sieved
½ CUP

In a small saucepan, melt butter over medium heat. Stir in parsley, lemon juice, onion, salt, and pepper. Cook, stirring constantly about 1 minute. Stir in bread crumbs and egg yolks.

DESSERT SAUCES

ORANGE SAUCE

This can be used instead of or in addition to whipped cream or sour cream atop an omelet. I sometimes add 2 tablespoons of orange liqueur, rum, or brandy. It's a favorite creation of my friends at Sunkist Growers, and who should know better?

1 cup sugar
5 tablespoons flour
⅛ teaspoon salt
Grated rind of 1 orange
½ cup fresh orange juice
Juice of ½ lemon
3 egg yolks
1 teaspoon butter
1 cup heavy cream, whipped

2½ CUPS

In heavy saucepan, mix together sugar, flour, and salt. Add rind, fruit juices, and egg yolks. Cook over low heat, stirring until thickened and smooth; add butter and cool. Fold in whipped cream.

LEMON SAUCE

I love this sauce with peaches, nectarines, apples, or pears. Goes great with mincemeat.

½ cup sugar
⅛ teaspoon salt
2 tablespoons cornstarch
1 cup boiling water
2 tablespoons butter
Juice of 1 lemon
1 teaspoon grated lemon rind

1¾ CUPS

In a heavy saucepan, mix together sugar, salt, and cornstarch. Gradually stir in boiling water. Cook, stirring constantly, until thickened. Remove from heat; stir in butter, lemon juice, and grated rind. Serve warm.

QUICKIE FRUIT SAUCE

Melt an 8-ounce jar of fruit preserves of your choice. Stir in 2 to 3 tablespoons rum, brandy, or fruit liquor.

Raspberry preserves are great with peaches or strawberries; blueberry with apples; apricot with pears; pineapple with bananas and coconut. Makes 1¼ cups.

FANCY WHIPPED CREAM

Fold 2 to 3 tablespoons liqueurs like Amaretto di Amore, Dutch Bittersweet Chocolate Liqueur, Kahlua or any fruit liqueur into 2 cups whipped cream. The sky's the limit.

PEANUT SAUCE

This is the peanut sauce that I use with a chocolate soufflé, but I found it's terrific served with banana, berry, or cherry omelets.

2 tablespoons sugar
2 tablespoons cornstarch
½ teaspoon salt
1 cup water
¼ cup coffee liqueur
½ cup coarsely chopped unsalted peanuts

1¾ CUPS

Mix sugar, cornstarch, and salt in saucepan. Stir in water gradually. Cook over medium heat, stirring constantly until mixture thickens and boils. Remove from heat; stir in liqueur and peanuts.

117

11.

How to Toss an Omelet-Making Party for Fun or Fund-raising

No one scores Brownie points making bologna sandwiches. Too bad! They'd be an easy out for entertaining.

But to be host with the most, you need something more than bologna. You need a specialty and you need money—two thoughts that worried me when I started going to other people's parties and chalking up social obligations that would have to be returned.

How?

Expertise is elusive when you need a road map to find the stove, as I did. As for money, with a family to support, I was closer to beer and burgers (no cachet at all) than I was to champagne and caviar. Even if I could have afforded the latter, why bother? There's no novelty in that kind of combination in New York social circles.

I wanted to be a *House and Garden* host whose parties were the talk of the town and I needed a gimmick. It was there all the time—but I couldn't see the omelets for the eggs. Frankly, omelets didn't occur to me because they were my bread and butter. I was making them coast to coast, promoting eggs and keeping every henhouse in the U.S. working overtime.

What's more, my idea of hosting a party is the kind of menu magic that leaves the host with nothing to do except enjoy.

KABOOM! The fondue fad pointed me in the right direction. The idea of black-tie guests all over town spearing bread cubes, dipping 'em into bubbling cheese, and loving every minute of it knocked me out.

Why do what everyone else was doing? Do something different. I'd go a step further than fondue and let guests cook their own omelets—no work for me except in the preparation stage.

The main course would be a fun-for-all floor show with everyone taking credit for culinary creativity and me taking credit for being so clever.

As a party idea, it couldn't miss. It was:

Easy.

Inexpensive.

Guaranteed to go over big.

The first one did, and so have the many (literally

hundreds) I've given since. Formal or informal, they've all been fun. Try my idea. You'll like it—your guests will too.

Do it for friends. Do it for fund-raising. Either way, you can't miss. The key to success is advance planning.

If you're looking to raise money for a worthy cause, pick a place that will accommodate a crowd, then check out essentials like the availability of butane burners or hot plates. If using the latter, make sure wiring's adequate so you don't blow a fuse.

Borrow as many burners and hot plates as you can. Ditto for Silverstone 10-inch omelet pans. Remember to figure rental cost or purchase price into your expenses so that when it comes to pricing tickets, you'll have a good margin of profit. Expenses also include food, postage, printing, and room rental but, if you play it smart, you can probably get the use of a hall free for a charitable event.

Publicity is important. A fund-raiser shouldn't be a secret. Remember, you want the world to know, so get the word around with a mailing to your group's membership, flyers posted prominently on supermarket bulletin boards, community centers and such. Let your local newspaper know, too, with a carefully worded press release that makes the event sound like too much fun to miss. Remember, an omelet-making party has lots of appeal.

It's a cooking lesson.

It's a meal.

It's a good time had by all.

Promote it properly and you'll get 'em all—even the

skinflints, who'll feel they'll be getting their money's worth. And they'll be right.

If you want more money jingling into the till, appoint a door-prize committee to make the rounds of local merchants, then sell tickets and raffle off what's donated. Look for omelet-related prizes—Silverstone pans, burners, ladles, wedges of cheese, mixing bowls, dinners for two at a local omelet restaurant. But no need to limit yourself. Take whatever's donated. The first rule of fund-raising: Never say "No" to anything that's free.

TIMETABLE FOR FUND-RAISER

1. Several months in advance, pick a place.
2. Several weeks before the event, mail invitations and get out publicity.
3. One to two weeks before, get a head count by tallying tickets sold.
4. One week in advance, make a shopping list and order food and supplies (see "Food Needed" chart).
5. Two to three days in advance, buy everything except perishables, which should be purchased the day before.
6. On the great day, set up tables and cooking stations four hours in advance of event.
7. Two to three hours before ticket holders troop in, get your committee to work chopping and preparing filling ingredients.

8. Half an hour before, get cracking with eggs, mixing them with water.

9. Arrange food at each station.

10. Welcome guests, demonstrate the easy art of omelet-making, and then on with the show and their individual efforts.

SUPPLIES FOR EACH STATION
(Plan on 1 station for each 10 to 15 guests.)

Whether 10 friends in your own cozy kitchen or 100 paying guests in the church hall are cooking omelets, here's what you'll need at *each* station:

1. A source of heat. For a large gathering you'll need a portable heat source for each station. A butane burner, electric hot plate or camp stove will work. Forget alcohol burners—they don't get hot enough. At home, your kitchen stove with the two front burners set on medium-high will work just fine. If using many portable burners, make sure there will be enough fuel or outlets. Always read and follow the directions for whatever heat source you're using. Some city ordinances don't allow open flame burners, so check this out in advance.

2. One omelet pan, 8 to 10 inches in diameter, that has a nonstick coating and sloping sides. Buy or borrow them for the event. If a fund-raiser, get them do-

nated by local housewares stores, then give them away as door prizes.

3. One butter plate and knife.

4. One nylon or plastic pancake turner placed at the right of each burner.

5. One ladle for each bowl of egg mixture. The marvel of omelet-making marvels is this: A standard kitchen ladle holds exactly ½ cup, the perfect amount of egg mixture for making 1 omelet.

6. One serving plate per person placed in a stack to the left of each burner.

7. Egg mixture (2 eggs, 2 tablespoons of water, and seasonings per omelet).

8. Assortment of fillings. The bowls or tureens filled with egg mixture can be shared by two stations.

You're not going to need as many stations as you might suppose because omelet-making goes fast. Even allowing for a little reluctance, lagging, ladling the mixture into the pan or hemming and hawing over the filling choices, the statistics speak for themselves: 1 omelet, 40 seconds; 10 omelets, less than 7 minutes. In other words, with 10 stations, you can move 100 people from omelet-making to eating in no more than 10 minutes. The incredible, edible egg is a wonder.

No need to fret about how much food you'll need. It's charted for you. In checking the chart, remember that amounts are for one type of filling used in an omelet; thus if you mix ham and mushrooms, you'll only need maybe half as much of each as is indicated.

When you're playing host to omelet-making friends,

stand around and offer suggestions. At a fund-raiser, spot committee members at each station to offer encouragement and/or advice.

WHAT MORE IS NEEDED

For a surefire success, round out the menu for an omelet-making party with a few additions. When I entertain, I like to serve asparagus or broccoli hollandaise—that fresh green makes a pretty contrast to a golden omelet.

At a fund-raiser, the easiest out is a salad. Maybe because ingredients can be tossed together before the crowd collects.

Be sure to include rolls (at home, nothing beats crusty French bread, toasted English muffins, or bagels). Serve coffee and dessert.

My dessert choice invariably is French pastry—not just because the French gave us the omelet, too, but because I can pick it up at the local patisserie. At a fund-raiser, coffee with cookies or cake is easiest.

When it comes to the extras, increase your profit at a fund-raiser by looking for donations. Get committee members to donate salads, breads, desserts; a local restaurant to provide the coffee. Consider opening the event with a wine-tasting, courtesy of your local liquor store.

When your fund-raiser is over, don't forget the most

important thing: Saying thanks to those who've made a contribution. Say it in writing with a personal letter. Say it in public next time your organization meets. Say it in a bulletin, if your organization publishes one, then make sure all concerned get a copy. Soften them all up for the encore omelet fund-raiser next year.

AMOUNT OF FOOD NEEDED*

NUMBER OF PERSONS	1	10	20	50	100
INGREDIENTS					
EGGS, Large	2	20	40	100	200
Shredded cheese	¼ to ⅓ cup or 1 to 1⅓ oz.	10 oz. to ¾ lb.	1¼ to 1½ lbs.	3 to 4 lbs.	6 to 8 lbs.
Cubed ham	¼ cup or 2⅔ oz.	1 to 2 lbs.	3½ to 4 lbs.	8¾ to 10 lbs.	17½ to 20 lbs.
Chopped onion	1 to 2 Tbsps.	¼ to ½ lb.	½ to 1 lb.	1¼ to 2½ lbs.	2½ to 5 lbs.
Bacon, cooked and crumbled	1 to 2 slices	½ to 1 lb.	1 to 2 lbs.	2½ to 5 lbs.	5 to 10 lbs.
Mushrooms, sliced, canned, drained	¼ cup	8 (4-oz.) cans	16 (4-oz.) cans	2 (68-oz.) cans	4 (68-oz.) cans
Green pepper, chopped	1 to 2 Tbsps.	¼ to ½ lb.	½ to 1 lb.	1¼ to 2½ lbs.	2½ to 5 lbs.
Vegetables, frozen, cooked, drained	2 oz.	2 (10-oz.) pkgs.	4 (10-oz.) pkgs.	10 (10-oz.) pkgs.	20 (10-oz.) pkgs.
Shrimp, cooked, deveined frozen, thawed	2 oz.	1¼ lbs.	2½ lbs.	6¼ lbs.	12½ lbs.

	2 Tbsps.	10 to 12 oz.	1 to 1½ lbs.	3½ lbs.	7 lbs.
Preserves or jam	2 Tbsps.	10 to 12 oz.	1 to 1½ lbs.	3½ lbs.	7 lbs.
Peaches, canned, sliced, drained	½ cup or 4 oz.	2½ lbs.	5 lbs.	12½ lbs.	25 lbs.
Sour cream or yogurt	¼ cup	2½ cups	5 cups	12½ cups	25 cups
Butter	1 Tbsp. or ½ oz.	½ cup + 2 Tbsps. or 1 stick + 2 Tbsps. or 5 oz.	1¼ cups or 2½ sticks or 10 oz.	3⅛ cups or 6¼ sticks or 1 lb. 9 oz.	6¼ cups or 12½ sticks or 3⅛ lbs.
Worcestershire	one bottle per two stations				
Hot pepper sauce	one bottle per two stations				
Salt/pepper	one set for each station				

*Note: The amounts above are for one type of food only in an omelet. Thus, if you mix ham and mushrooms, you'll need a total of ¼ cup, or half as much of each.

The range in the amounts of ingredients varies to allow you to choose the type of omelet you like best. If the people in your group want hearty, generously filled omelets, buy the amount listed for the most filling. If smaller omelets are what you like, then buy the smaller amount listed on the range. And, of course, if middle-of-the-road is the choice, then buy a moderate amount, following the range on the chart.

Index

Beans, green, 49, 53, 63
Béchamel sauce, 105
Beef, 47–48
  and chili, 67
  corned, 49–50, 65
  ground, 63
Blue cheese and olive sauce, 105
Blueberries, 42
Brandy, 72, 76, 80, 115
  apricot, 72
Breakfast omelets, 40–44
British omelets, 62
Broccoli, 48
  and turkey in hollandaise, 58
Broiling, 78
Brunch omelets, 40–44
Butterscotch chips, 76

Cabbage, red, 63
Cake, 80
Calories, 59
Cantonese lobster sauce, 110
Caraway seeds, 49
Carrots, 48, 49, 57, 58
Casere cheese, 42
Caviar, 68
Celery, 58
Cereal flakes, 73
Cheddar cheese, 49, 82, 85
  and apples, 72
  and bacon, 49
  and chives, 49
  and olives, 55

  and pears, 77
  and sausage, 43
Cheese, 40, 48, 55, 57, 58.
  See also individual names
  sauce, 102, 111
  and sausage, 43
  and tomato sauce, 104
Cherries, 73, 76
Cherry Heering, 73
Chervil, 58
Chicken:
  and chutney with nuts, 65
  creamed, 49
  à la King sauce, 104
  livers, 52
  with tomatoes and rice, 69
Chili, 67
  sauce, Sloppy Joe, 111
Chilies, green, 67
Chinese omelets, 52, 62, 92–96
Chives, 41, 49, 58
Chocolate chips, 76
Chop suey, 62
Chow mein, 62
Chutney, 65
Cinnamon, 63, 78
Clams, 49
Cloves, 68
Coconut, 65, 73, 76
Compote, 96
Corn, 67
Corned beef, 49–50, 65
Cottage cheese, 41
Crab, 50, 67, 106